SPEECH ACTS and LITERARY THEORY

Speech Acts
and Literary
Theory

Sandy Petrey

Routledge

NEW YORK   LONDON

For Charlotte and Donald

Published in 1990 by

Routledge
An imprint of Routledge, Chapman and Hall, Inc.
29 West 35 Street
New York, NY 10001

Published in Great Britain by

Routledge
11 New Fetter Lane
London EC4P 4EE

Library of Congress Cataloging in Publication Data

Petrey, Sandy.
    Speech acts and literary theory / Sandy Petrey.
      p.   cm.
    Includes bibliographical references.
    ISBN 0-415-90181-2 ISBN 0-415-90182-0 (pbk.)
    1. Speech acts (Linguistics)   2. Literature—Philosophy.
    I. Title.
    P95.55.P48   1990
    306.4'4—dc20   90-35000

British Library Cataloguing in Publication Data

Petrey, Sandy
    Speech acts and literary theory.
    1. Linguistics. Theories
    I. Title
    410.1

    ISBN 0-415-90181-2
    ISBN 0-415-90182-0 pbk

Contents

Acknowledgments

In different form, I discussed some of the topics addressed here in articles published in *Philosophy and Social Criticism* and *Texte*. I am happy to express my gratitude to the journals' editors.

Part I

Beginnings

1

Saying versus Doing

Twentieth-century literary theory has consistently explored the implications of the simple fact that literature consists of language. Inquiry into the nature and function of language outside literature has furnished the conceptual basis for many hugely influential efforts to develop guiding principles for apprehending the nature and function of the literary text. The axioms of structuralism, transformational grammar, and other linguistic schools have been applied to literary analysis with remarkable results, and almost all recent philosophies of language have become the armature of a philosophy of literature as well.

This book examines the implications for literary study of J. L. Austin's philosophy of language, speech-act theory. While application of Austin's work to the critical enterprise certainly continues the fruitful adaptations of language study characteristic of modern literary scholarship, however, speech-act theory challenges a foundational principle of other linguistic schools. It shifts attention from what language *is* to what it *does* and sees a *social process* where other linguistic philosophies see a *formal structure*. From a speech-act perspective, all linguistic artifacts, including those that count as literary, must be understood in relation to the sociohistorical context of their production and reception. Since Ferdinand de Saussure first recognized that language is a form not a substance, linguistic research has focused on the abstract features language displays regardless of where and when it's used. Speech-act theory addresses rather language's productive force, which depends entirely on where and when it's used. Other linguistic schools address the structure of language in itself; speech-act theory examines the power of language in communities.

Language's communal power is the effect of its "performative" capacity, a concept Austin systematically explained in the book entitled *How to Do Things with Words*. Austin's title is an excellent summary of his concept. The major purpose of the 1955 Harvard lectures that became *How to Do Things with Words* was to show that words are not only something we use to *say* things. We also use them to *do* things, and the difference between saying and doing is of such magnitude that we must understand the two functions in distinct ways. "Performative" was Austin's term for language with the primary function of doing something, "constative" his term for language used primarily for saying something.

To appreciate the difference between constative and performative language, imagine a friend who walks in as you're reading this paragraph and looks quizzically at your book. You respond by saying "I bought it yesterday" or "I don't know what I think about it, I just started." In both cases, you're using words to say something, to tell your friend what you did or how you feel. Your language is therefore constative. It remains constative even if you're lying through your teeth and actually stole the book last month and are now reading it for the third time. Statements may be true or they may be false, but so long as they at least purport to describe reality they remain constative.

Now change the scenario. Assume you and your friend are taking a speed-reading course, and you respond to the quizzical look by saying "I bet you ten dollars I can read this in an hour." Your friend checks the number of pages and says "You're on." Both "I bet" and "You're on" are performative rather than constative. Together the two utterances constitute a bet and obligate the loser to pay ten dollars to the winner. These words do things, they perform an action, their articulation is a creation. If they aren't spoken, no bet is made. Whereas your constative descriptions of when you bought this book and how long you've been reading it don't affect the facts to which you refer, the performative "I bet" and "You're on" literally produce—*perform*—the bet. Constative utterances describe the world, performative utterances become part of the world.

Change the scenario further. Imagine different ways the bet can be made. Say you and your friend are quite competitive about who does better in the speed-reading course. Each of you continually strives to read faster than the other, each is always ready to bet ten dollars on success. In that case, your friend might simply remind you of the speed you have to beat, "Fifteen hundred words a minute." By the understanding between you, that laconic statistic could constitute a ten-dollar bet and set you off to finish the book at a speed of fifteen hundred and fifty words a minute under penalty of paying up if you fail. Although the word "bet" wasn't spoken, the words that were nevertheless constituted a bet and thus fulfilled a performative function.

There's no limit on kinds of bets or words that might be used to make them. The scenarios I suggested could be extended at will, but they all have to display one essential feature. *Both* you and your friend must understand and accept that a bet has been made. There is no bet—and therefore no performative—if recognition of the bet is limited to one of you. This condition is so vital that "recognition of the bet is limited to one of you" is a patent absurdity. A bet limited to one is simply not there to be recognized. Like all performative language, that used to make a bet derives the whole of its force from collective acceptance. The collectivity can be as small as two people, but performative speech can never be the unilateral act of a single individual. If I could make bets by myself, my gambling income would very soon amount to all the money in the world.

Common recognition that the bet is made can be explicit ("I bet" and "you're on") or implicit ("fifteen hundred words a minute" or "okay"). The point of consequence is that the recognition must be common. Whatever words you use to make your bet, you haven't made it unless those words are understood and accepted as a bet by the person to whom you say them.

The absolute necessity of communicative success for the performative to exist is in fact one of the most striking distinctions between it and the constative. If you say to a third person, "My friend and I have a running ten-dollar bet on who can read faster," you've produced a constative utterance regardless of whether the person hears you. In direct contrast, you must have what Austin called audience uptake if "I bet you ten dollars I can read faster" is to be performative.

While the possibility of total uptake is always problematic, when the performative is at issue there's a practical lower limit below which words cannot fall and still do things. Collective accord is requisite as well as prerequisite to words' ability to do things, which is why Austin considered adopting the word "contractual" instead of inventing the word "performative."

The performative's dependence on multilateral participation is especially obvious with bets. As Austin put it,

> To bet is not, as I pointed out in passing, merely to utter the words "I bet, &c.": someone might do that all right, and yet we might still not agree that he had in fact, or at least entirely, succeeded in betting. To satisfy ourselves of this, we have only, for example, to announce our bet after the race is over. (13–14) (All quotations in my first two chapters are from *How to Do Things with Words*, Austin 1962.)

If you follow up on the announcement by telling those around you to pay the handsome sum you just won, their reaction will be a memorable lesson on the performative's need for multilateral understanding.

"Hold on! Can't people make bets with themselves?" Of course. I do it all the time. But when I do, my bets aren't an instance of Austin's performatives, which have to encompass more than one person. The standard introductions to speech acts start with the promise, and the reason I chose bets instead is that the difference between bets imagined and bets performed is probably clearer than that between promises we make to ourselves and to others. In my head I can indeed make my bet after the race is over.

The bet makes it more apparent, but the difference between performative and imaginative, which is also the difference between the collective and the personal, is critical to *all* speech acts. Austin in fact chose the promise to make the point,

> It is obviously necessary that to have promised I must normally
> (A) have been *heard* by someone, perhaps the promisee;
> (B) have been understood by him as promising. (22)

Much of the excitement of speech-act theory is its demonstration that entities often taken as incompatible are instead thoroughly interactive. Words and things, speaking and doing are one and the same when language performs. The theory also brings together the inner self and the outer world, the individual and the communal, but it does so only when we participate *perceptibly* in communal life. Speech-act theory doesn't have anything to say about the promises we make to ourselves because, not being speech, they aren't acts either.

Austin codified the primacy of the collective in several ways, most strikingly in the precondition for performative language he labeled Rule A.1: "There must exist an accepted conventional procedure having a certain conventional effect, that procedure to include the uttering of certain words by certain persons in certain circumstances" (14). The repeated "conventional" and the redundant "accepted" all designate the same necessity for communal agreement. As its etymology specifies—*convenire* means "to come together, to convene"—a convention exists by virtue of trans-individual ratification. Part of what's accepted in any convention is that more than one person is doing the acceptance. Words do things in a social setting, and Austin made sociality so prominent in Rule A.1 because it's the foundation on which every other rule is erected.

Austin gives letters and numbers to five other rules besides A.1. The capital distinctions among them will be discussed later. But all five are a logical consequence of the requirement for a conventional procedure with conventional effect. Rule A.2 says that the people and circumstances involved must be those specified by the convention, for instance, while the other four rules say that the procedure and its participants must perform as the convention dictates. Rule A.1 is primary not only because it's the precondition for the others but also because the last five make its implications explicit. Before there can be performative language, there must exist a social body that recognizes and accepts the conventional procedure in which the language functions. For the language to function successfully, a social body must apprehend it in the same way.

Betting was one of the four examples Austin used to introduce performative speech in the first of the twelve lectures collected in *How to Do Things with Words*. But another of the four introductory examples, the marriage ceremony, has become the most broadly cited illustration of what Austin had in mind. Betting is a relatively loose convention that can operate when its actualization is known to no one except the two bettors. Marriage, far more public and structured, normally entails a rigidly defined set of words, and in our society it always requires official inscription in compliance with strict communal protocols. Marriage thus demonstrates the collective nature of the performative with great clarity. Moreover, social enforcement of the responsibilities imposed by marriage vividly demonstrates the importance collectivities attach to the things done by the words they empower to act. Welshing on a bet with a friend doesn't ordinarily subject you to the police power of the state. Welshing on a marriage by taking a second spouse can land you in jail.

To exemplify the words spoken to enter into marriage, Austin used a phrase that is the performative at its most lapidary, "I do." When you say "I do" during the marriage ceremony, you do what you say you do by saying nothing more than "I do." For several reasons, however, "I now pronounce you husband and wife" has become the marriage performative of choice among speech-act theorists. "I do" is part of an ongoing series of active utterances, whereas "I now pronounce you husband and wife" declares that the series is completed, that the marriage has taken place.

What does it mean to say "the marriage has taken place?" As always, the first and most important condition is described in Rule A.1. For there to be a marriage, there must exist a conventional procedure known as marriage with conventional effects accepted by the newlyweds and their fellow citizens. Moreover, the conditions imposed by the conventional procedure—the qualifications participants must display, the words they must utter, the documents they must complete—all have to be met in the prescribed manner.

Together such conditions illustrate the extent to which marriage involves the body politic in a way that betting may not. Each component of the marriage ceremony is prescribed in advance, each must be performed as prescribed for "I now pronounce you husband and wife" to do what it says. Although we can imagine betting conventions limited to the performative minimum of two people, marriage in our society demands a far more extensive collective involvement. If I want to make a bet, all I need is one person to take it. If I want to get married, I must have not only someone to marry but also prior social codification of what's required of us and subsequent social recognition that we said and did the right things.

Other performatives entail even greater social participation. When a president issues a declaration of war, when an ayatollah designates God's enemies, when a generalissimo proclaims a state of siege, when a junta abrogates the constitution, the things words do are directly endured as well as indirectly ratified by the members of a speech-act community. Conventional procedures can result in seizure of your property and your person as well as your surrender or acceptance of a ten-dollar bill. There's a huge difference between the judicial performatives "Case dismissed" and "Twenty years."

A wager, a marriage, and a declaration of war furnish a reasonable spectrum of the scope and impact of performative language. The things done by words in the three cases range from acceptance of a (perhaps) trivial obligation by two individuals to the massive redeployment of the resources and population of a nation state. But from one end of the performative spectrum to the other, words derive their power to produce what they say from the conventional procedures accepted by a definite collectivity.

By virtue of their absolute dependence on communal conventions, we must evaluate words that do things through procedures different from those applied to words that only say things. With the performative, knowledge of communal conventions is at least as important as the ability to understand what's said. Think about the difference between "I now pronounce you husband and wife" and an ordinary constative: "The words in this sentence are printed in black ink against a background of white paper." To say whether the constative sentence is true or false, you need only look at the words and paper that are the sentence's *referents*, the things its words are saying something about (and not doing anything to). As it happens, the statement is true. But again your procedure would be the same even if it were false. "The words in this sentence are printed in orange ink against a background of green paper" is constative even though inaccurate. Our ability to discern its inaccuracy requires nothing more than an understanding of English color terms and an eyesight capable of distinguishing what they designate.

Something other than lexical and perceptive competence is required to know whether "I now pronounce you husband and wife" produces a married couple, however. We must also be familiar with a conventional procedure and know whether the conditions it specifies have been met. The appearances in this book of "I now pronounce you husband and wife" haven't actually pronounced anyone husband and wife. You can read the sentence aloud as often as you want, but in all probability it still won't institute a couple's married life. The reason is obviously not the words themselves (in other circumstances they do indeed count; ask anyone who's been through a difficult divorce) nor in our understanding of them. Lacking when I write and you read "I now pronounce you husband and wife" are the many other components of the convention of marriage as our society has constituted it: a couple with certain qualifications, an officiating individual with certain other qualifications, and so forth. To know whether a constative description is true, we need only perceive referents and compare them to words. To know whether a marriage has been performed, or a bet has been made, or war has been declared, we must also know the conventions observed by a community where the words were spoken.

Say I turn to my wife in a public place and yell "I divorce you! I divorce you! I divorce you!" Are we divorced? The answer depends wholly on time and place. In the United States of America in the twentieth century, although I may not have contributed to the warmth of spousal feelings, I haven't at all affected the condition inaugurated by the performative language at my wedding. In another time and place, however, a triple "I divorce you!" could have exactly the same force of dissolution as a judge's "Divorce is hereby pronounced" here and now. Like every other performative, the language dissolving or effecting a marriage can't be understood except in connection to its social context.

That context is consequently a vital constituent of any attempt to apprehend an utterance's performative strength. Again the difference from the constative is stark. I have been married twice, in wholly dissimilar circumstances. The first time was in a church in Alabama in the presence of hundreds of relatives and guests at a ceremony conducted by a male pastor proud of his elocutionary prowess with the liturgy favored by the Southern Baptist Convention. The second time was at the home of a female Justice of the Peace in New Hampshire; there were no guests or witnesses, and the JP had difficulty finding as well as reading the ceremony prescribed by the New Hampshire civil code. Represented constatively, the two weddings have nothing in common except my presence. Contemplated performa-

tively, they are identical. Both conformed to the procedures established by my society for producing a marriage, both had the effect of
changing my condition from that of a bachelor to that of a husband.
The objective circumstances were incommensurable, the performative force indistinguishable.

How to Do Things with Words devotes a lot of intellectual and rhetorical energy to combating the belief that language's value is determined uniquely by its connection to or disconnection from objective
reality. For the viewpoints Austin grouped and dismissed as the "descriptive fallacy," the interest in verbal representations of my two
weddings would be that a different reality produced a different discourse, that changes in the referent elicited changes in language. With
truth the sole concern, the *force* of the words performing the marriage
drops from sight. Austin: "It was for too long the assumption of philosophers that the business of a 'statement' can only be to 'describe' some
state of affairs, or to 'state some fact,' which it must do either truly
or falsely" (1). A principal purpose of the idea of the performative is
showing that assumption to be very wrong.

Dismissal of the belief that language's true or false description
of external reality constitutes its paramount identity has weighty
consequences for literary study. One of the great problems for critics
interested in relating literary language to other linguistic forms is
that other forms usually do indeed describe some state of affairs either
truly or falsely; yet the great bulk of literary language isn't descriptive
in the same sense. Take the famous words opening the last chapter of
Jane Eyre, "Reader, I married him." The pronouns in that sentence,
"I" and "him," refer to Jane and Rochester, which is to say that they
have no "referents" outside the book in which they appear. They
therefore belong with the forms of literary language dissociated from
what Austin called the "business" of stating some fact either truly or
falsely.

But the *verb* in "Reader, I married him" strongly reminds us that
stating some fact isn't the only business language accomplishes. Marriage is a ceremony performed by words, which also perform novels
and the characters within them. The referent of "I now pronounce you
husband and wife," *conventional* rather than objective, comes to be
through the agreements observed by a certain sociolinguistic community. Comparable conventional agreements produce fictional characters and their fictional world. To read a work of imaginative literature
is to encounter words that do things through processes like those
allowing all other performative language to produce what it names.
Jane and Rochester exist solely within language, but one of Austin's
capital lessons for literary criticism is that entities with purely linguis-

tic existence figure among the major constituents of collective existence. Like marriage, Jane Eyre, Mr. Rochester, and their numberless imaginary fellows are the conventional effect of a conventional procedure.

We'll return to the ways a speech-act perspective on literary works challenges the standard concept of fictional non-reference. For the present, what matters is that Austin's vision of the performative challenges the concept of the referent in non-fictional language as well. That concept, most plausible when speech is constative, holds that words and things, language and its referent, are unproblematically distinct from one another. With a constative utterance—"The cat is on the mat" was Austin's favorite example—words name and describe things independent of their names and descriptions. If we want to know whether the cat is on the mat, we look at the cat, the mat, and the physical relationship between them. In each segment of that operation, words and referents stand absolutely apart. The relationship between the referents holds whether the words are spoken or not; the cat's on the mat regardless of whether anyone says so. As a consequence, the words can be altered and reordered ("the mat is on the cat") without affecting the things named. With constative language, words and referents are distinct and distinctive.

With the performative, however, the referent is *within* the words and the conventional procedure they enact. To say "I bet ten dollars" isn't to describe but to *make* a bet. Because the referent doesn't exist without the words, altering the words ("I bet ten cents") alters the referent as well. In contrast to a cat or a mat, a bet (a promise, a marriage, a declaration of war) has no existence outside of language and the force its users assign it. You can't separate a bet from what's said about it because it and what's said are one and the same. The reality of a cat, a mat, and their physical relationship doesn't come from social conventions. The reality of a speech act *is* a social convention.

While we may well ask if a constative description is right or wrong, truth and falsity are beside the point when we consider a performative action. Constative truth depends on the harmony between a verbal utterance and a non-verbal condition. If the cat is on the mat, then "the mat is on the cat" is false. But a successful performative is *necessarily* in harmony with a non-verbal condition. When a government says "The constitution is suspended," it makes no sense to talk about the truth of the government's statement because non-verbal reality—suspension of the constitution and of the civil rights it protects—isn't represented but produced by the government's decree. After the constitution is suspended, there are normally glaring newspaper headlines repeating that *The Constitution is Suspended*. We might wonder whether the headlines are accurate, but in the governmental declaration those same words unfortunately do not allow doubt.

Imagine a courtroom in which a trial is being televised. At a certain moment, an officer of the court strides before the bench and announces that court is now in session. Immediately, a reporter in a glass booth at the rear of the room repeats the officer's words into a microphone. In one case, the beginning of the court's official session is *effected*; in the other, it's *stated*. In one case, the words are performative; in the other, the same words are constative. Because it represents a referent, a constative utterance can be evaluated as correct or incorrect; because it enacts a referent, a performative utterance can't be so evaluated. The possibility of truth depends on the possibility of falseness, and successfully performative language cannot be true for the compelling reason that it cannot be false.

What do we ask about the performative if we aren't concerned with its truth? The answer is implicit in the adjective I've been applying throughout this discussion, *successful*. While words that say things are either right or wrong, words that do things are either successful or unsuccessful—in Austin's terminology, they're either felicitous or infelicitous, happy or unhappy. An escapee from the adjoining jail who steps in front of the judge's bench and pronounces court in session has not told a lie but produced an infelicitous declaration. A stranger who says "I now pronounce you husband and wife" to two people, each married to someone else, neither with the intention of marrying the other, has violated not truth but a conventional procedure. Words do things when they felicitously invoke a convention, and their infelicitous failure to do things signals a breakdown of the convention (not) being applied.

The concept of an utterance's felicity is closely connected to what Austin called illocutionary force. Appearance of "The constitution is suspended" in a governmental decree and in a newspaper, like a court officer's and a television reporter's "Court is now in session," provide examples of a single *locution* with vastly different *illocutionary* force. The same words with the same meaning—the same locutions—have different conventional powers, and one of the most important principles of speech-act theory is that such difference of powers is at least as important in analyzing language as lexical and semantic identity. We can say a very great deal about words taken in and of themselves, as locutions. To say something interesting or useful about their illocutionary force, however, we must look at the conventions invoked by their use and their users.

Conventions' active presence in illocutionary language is the reason speech-act theory must always move beyond the formal analysis practiced by other linguistic schools. Locutionary *form* is complete and whole *within* the linguistic utterance; illocutionary *force* is a combination of language and social practice. If I want to analyze any of the purely linguistic properties of a constative utterance like "The cat is on the mat," it's both pointless and distracting for me to inquire into the utterance's referents (is the cat actually on the mat?) or the situation of its production (who said this under what circumstances?). Grammar, semantics, phonetic and graphematic systems—locutionary rather than illocutionary properties—are all right there in the words themselves.

What's pointless and distracting for understanding language as *locution*, however, is obligatory for understanding *illocution*. It's impossible to know whether a performative works without situating it. The only way to decide whether "I bet ten dollars" performs a bet is to relate the words to the betting conventions observed in the circumstances where the utterance is produced.

Illocution is to locution as speech acts are to speech. Each formulation distinguishes what words say as words from what they do as a component of human interaction; each contrasts the social focus of Austin's concern to the abstract structure of language in itself. Whereas Rule A.1 establishes the collective preconditions for the performative, the categories of felicity and illocutionary force address the collective circumstances permitting the performative actually to act.

Speech-act theory brings illocution to the fore by situating language within the relationships lived by its users. Twentieth-century linguistics has been largely characterized by concentration on the internal features that allow language to convey a meaning. Austin shifts attention to the things language does other than convey a meaning. As a formal locution, language stands apart from society; it becomes a pragmatic illocution within society. Illocutionary identity consists solely of language's function within the conventional interactions that characterize a given sociohistorical group.

In many cases—"*I bet* ten dollars," "*I now pronounce* you husband and wife"—illocutionary identity is specified as a performative utterance is made. "I bet" and "I pronounce" simultaneously name a convention and apply it. This kind of explicit performative is common: "I *warn* you that he's got a nasty temper;" "I *swear* I'll finish next week." So frequent is a first-person pronoun with a present-indicative verb in performative utterances that Austin and other theorists have tried to set such a pronoun-verb combination as the performative's defining feature. Even when, as in a junta's "The constitution is suspended," the pronoun-verb combination is not explicit, it can readily be supplied: "*We declare* that the constitution is suspended."

Despite its broad applicability, there are important exceptions to this rule. Think about the insult. When I say something offensive about your intelligence, your courage, your hygienic standards, or your mother's sexual availability, I am in dangerous ways using words to do things rather than to say things. The *truth* of my insulting words is irrelevant to their *force*, and as a consequence I've produced a classic example of performative as opposed to constative speech. Yet I can't convert my insult into a sentence beginning with a first-person pronoun and a verb in the present indicative that names my speech act. "I insult you that you smell bad" comes closer to undoing than to expressing the illocutionary force of the insulting words alone. "You stink" is an insult; "I insult you" is just weird.

While Austin and his followers devoted much speculative effort to defining the performative in purely locutionary terms, they never succeeded. As the insult invalidates the criterion of first-person pronoun and performative verb, so other active utterances have continually refuted efforts to categorize performative language on the basis of the language alone. The problems Austin described in 1955 remain imposing obstacles to a purely locutionary approach several decades later. "Now we failed to find a grammatical criterion for performatives, but we thought that perhaps we could insist that every performative *could* be in principle put into the form of an explicit performative [. . .] Since then we have found, however, that it is often not easy to be sure that, even when it is apparently in explicit form, an utterance is performative or that it is not" (91). The difference between locutionary identity and illocutionary force has as corollary that no abstract representation of any utterance can satisfactorily define the concrete act it performs.

Speech versus acts, saying versus doing, meaning versus performing, structure versus practice, locution versus illocution: every pair opposes language in itself to language in context, for context alone determines the conventional effects produced by an utterance governed by Rule A.1. This is best seen by considering the vast number of illocutionary conventions that can be activated by a single locution. "The window's open" could *warn* you to be careful not to fall out, *request* you to close it, *inform* you of a state of affairs, *guess* about a state of affairs, *contradict* your idea of a state of affairs, and on and on. The words in the locution are always the same, but the illocutionary acts they accomplish vary. Whereas locutions are purely linguistic, illocutions are something more. The distinction is even clearer when we act it out.

Read this paragraph carefully. Every author has a right to expect that of a reader.

Read this paragraph carefully. If you pay attention now, the rest of the book will be far easier.

Read this paragraph carefully. It's short and simple enough so even you might be able to get it.

Read this paragraph carefully. I think you'll find it helpful as you go farther into Austin's thought.

A demand, a promise, an insult, a suggestion: "Read this paragraph carefully" can have all those illocutionary definitions and many more. The reason no set of linguistic characteristics can define the performative is that every set of linguistic units can perform in multiple ways. To understand what words say, we can look only at the words. To understand what they do, we must also look at their users.

Insults, suggestions, threats, demands, and other performatives are defined by the community in which the action is accomplished, not by some universal and eternal idea of what the action is. Social interaction, the convening evoked in the etymology and ontology of conventions, determines just what it is that words do as well as making it possible for them to do anything at all.

As Austin often repeated, "we must notice that the illocutionary act is a conventional act: an act done as conforming to a convention" (105). In order to know to which convention the illocutionary act is conforming, you must also know in which community it's being performed. Illocutionary force varies with the collectivity that produces it. A sentence expressing admiration in one group—"She's very feminine" or "He's very masculine," for instance—can express contempt in another; a compliment and an insult can differ solely in the time and place in which the same words in the same sequence are spoken. Painstakingly accurate descriptions of the formal linguistic structure that constitutes locution help not at all if my interests are illocutionary; satisfying those illocutionary· interests squarely confronts me with the social being of a social whole.

The conventional context dominating inquiry into the illocutionary force of performative utterances must not be confused with the physical context so often crucial to the descriptive accuracy of constative utterances. Austin sometimes used "descriptive" and "constative" interchangeably because the constative's defining function is representing objective reality, something quite different from the performative's production of social reality. The constative's referent is outside it, the performative's within it. If I say "The window's open" constatively, looking at the window allows you to know all you need to about whether I'm correct. But if I say the same thing performatively, then you must know the social convention in operation to tell whether I'm making a request, issuing a warning, or venturing a guess. Whether my description of the window is true is certainly not the main point if I'm speaking performatively, and in some speech acts the question of truth can't even arise. When I say, "I guess the window's open," my guess stays a guess in complete disregard for the condition of the window. The performative's invariable conventional ground means that it can have vertiginously variable connections to an objective situation.

There are clearly objective situations that constrict illocutionary possibilities. If you're sitting on a fortieth-story window sill snorting a white powder and beginning to nod off, then my "The window's open" is quite likely to be a warning. But even such situations fail to diminish the conventional status of illocutionary identity. It's not an objective state of affairs but a shared understanding that makes "The window's open" equivalent to "I warn you you're about to splatter your brains all over the sidewalk"; no constative description of any given state of affairs can explain how this equivalency is established or maintained. Because it depends absolutely on conventional protocols, the performative is never available for infra- or ultra-conventional apprehension.

Austin's category of "perlocutionary" consequences—what happens *after* utterance of an illocution—was one of the ways he distinguished the performative's sheerly conventional being from objective situations. Go back to the fortieth-story window sill. You can respond to "The window's open" either by snorting where you are or by moving away. Both are perlocutionary responses, and neither has any effect on the illocutionary status of the words spoken to you. You were indeed warned even though you ignore the warning, fall over backwards, and take the ultimate perlocutionary step of in fact splattering your brains all over the sidewalk.

Any other performative can illustrate the illocutionary/perlocutionary distinction. A bet remains a bet even if the loser doesn't pay the winner; to welsh on a bet doesn't unmake it. If I promise to be on time, the illocutionary status of my promise is unaltered even if my perlocutionary behavior is to arrive several hours late. When the generalissimo felicitously suspends the constitution, it's suspended even if a perlocutionary uprising hangs the generalissimo. Although perlocutionary events can ignore or undo as well as affirm the things done by words, the words' illocutionary status is unaffected if the convention is observed when the words are spoken.

Again Austin makes the point emphatically and repetitively: "Illocutionary acts are conventional acts: perlocutionary acts are *not* conventional" (121). The future state of the world has no purchase on the force of my performative intervention in the world. Like any other component of collective interaction, conventions are subject to failure and revocation. But the convention presently in place determines the things words do regardless of its subsequent fate.

In the locution/illocution/perlocution triad, Austin's attention was uniformly on the middle term. "Our interest in these lectures is essentially to fasten on the second, illocutionary act and contrast it with the other two" (103). That dual contrast illuminates the capital difference between Austin and alternative visions of language. By rejecting the locution, Austin was refusing all purely verbal approaches, all definitions of linguistic form and structure that ignore how language operates in the world. By rejecting the perlocution, he was refusing all concepts of language as a secondary, derivative tool presenting the sole interest of its capacity to (mis)represent an extra-linguistic fact. To concentrate on locution is to make language all-important; to concentrate on perlocution is to make what's not language all-important. Austin's determination to "fasten" on the illocution made it possible for him to bring together what others keep apart.

For *contrasting* illocution to locution and perlocution does not at all imply *excluding* the linguistic or non-linguistic from consideration. Austin's philosophy is on the contrary a protest *against* exclusion, as is manifest in the two nouns that come together to name speech-act theory. The theory's purpose is to bring speech and acts together—or rather, to recognize that the many ways they're already together make it illegitimate to suppose that we can best understand them in isolation. As a locution, "The window's open" furnishes material for semantic, phonetic, syntactic, and graphematic exegesis with real theoretical importance. As a perlocution, falling forty stories to the sidewalk gives the most effective crash course imaginable in the brutality of brute facts. To fasten on the illocution is to refuse to let either of those alternatives take the stage alone, however compelling they may be.

Things done by words are no less things for their verbal provenance, and Austin often hedged on the nature of the dividing line between the illocutionary and perlocutionary realms. On the one hand, Lecture VIII informs us that "there is clearly a difference between what we feel to be the real production of real effects and what we regard as mere conventional consequences" (103). Yet Lecture X parenthetically assimilates the facts of real effects to the facts of conventional effects. There the illocutionary "act is constituted not by intention or by fact, essentially but by convention (which is of course a fact)" (128). What was "clearly a difference" between the factual and the conventional turns out to be not clear at all when a convention "is of course a fact."

Disconcerting as it can be, Austin's ambivalence about the factuality of conventions and the reality of their consequences doesn't affect his theory's global redefinition of the referent. Inherited ideas about the sign/referent dichotomy—the reliable distinction between words and things—continue to trouble even the man whose recognition that words do things actually makes signs and referents inextricable. Austin's sensitivity to illocutionary force occasionally gave way before nostalgia for the descriptive fallacy's certainty that the referent is uninvolved in what's said about it, that "*mere* conventional consequences" are somehow less than factual. In Austin's work as a whole, however, the factual and the conventional, the real and the verbal, come together as firmly and as productively as speech and acts. The social reality of conventional effects is no less consequential than the objective reality of things in themselves.

The effects produced by a felicitous "I now pronounce you husband and wife" are apparent, are indeed one of the dominant realities in our society. Although the distinction between getting married and getting hit in the head is certainly that between the conventional and the non-conventional, is one more real than the other? As far as magnitude of effect goes, marriage can hold its own with any number of purely physical, non-conventional occurrences.

Analogously, declaring war and making war are vastly different, and it's often appropriate to categorize the differences as those between what Austin called "the real production of real effects" and what he considered "mere conventional consequences." But it's hard to see why a declaration of war should be set absolutely apart from the perlocutionary acts of war that it initiates. The basis of the distinction, though conceptually crystal-clear, is existentially blurry. While the illocutionary force of a declaration of war may well be independent of the perlocutionary event of a bombing raid, it wouldn't be fun to explain to the families of the raid's victims that the declaration was a "mere convention."

Death, the ultimate non-conventional event, eradicates all possibility of participation in collective procedures. Again, however, it isn't obvious that we should demarcate certain deaths from a jury's classically performative "We find the defendant guilty" and a judge's equally classic "I sentence you to be hanged by the neck until dead." Such utterances possess their illocutionary force solely through the conventions codified in Rule A.1, but it's still silly to cut them off from the non-conventional death that follows them. Like war, death is such an overpowering physical reality that it seems obscene to compare it to the conventional reality underlying speech-act theory. Yet like a declaration of war, a condemnation to death is a speech act that can't be convincingly separated from the events it authorizes. Illocutionary force, a purely conventional creation, is not a reality if we oppose the real and the conventional. Yet illocutionary force is eminently a *force*; the conventional creations of collective interaction dominate the lived experience of every one of the interaction's participants.

This domination begins at birth, with establishment of identity through the performative act of baptism or some other rite of naming. It concludes with death; the end of social coexistence comes through the end of existence itself. From beginning to end, the human condition is shaped by the conventions activated and manifested by performative speech. To contemplate the human condition is to confront language in action, and there's paltry purpose in pretending that we can most efficaciously apprehend language and action by separating each from the other.

The principal consequence of Austin's decision to fasten on illocution is to incorporate language into the constitutive, shaping features of our lives. This integration of language into life proceeds irresistibly from speech-act theory's integration of language into society. Foregrounding the performative over the constative simultaneously emphasizes the collective over the formal and the community over the referent. Although language can always be apprehended either in itself or as a representation of what's outside it, Austin's concentration on illocutionary force precludes both of these escapes from language's *participation* in what's outside it, from its *creative use* of its formal structure. "An effect must be achieved on the audience if the illocutionary act is to be carried out [. . .] the performance of an illocutionary act involves the securing of *uptake*" (116–17). As a result, every approach to the illocutionary act confronts you with interaction between individuals within a social matrix. Because Rule A.1 is the performative's primary condition of possibility, to study the performative is also to confront the collective being that gives conventional effect to conventional procedures.

The constative refers to things impervious to the truth or falsity of their verbal description, the performative to entities created or obliterated by verbal felicity. With constative language, the referent is an independent entity. With performative language, it's always a precise community as well. "What we do import by the use of the nomenclature of illocution is a reference [. . .] to the conventions of illocutionary force as bearing on the special circumstances of the occasion of the issuing of the utterance" (115). Because performative language does things through communal empire over the circumstances in which it acts, a community and its conventions must figure in any discussion of how to do things with words.

A last gambling scenario: you won the bets you made with your friend at the beginning of this book, but instead of ten-dollar bills you got various explanations of why you weren't going to be paid. If your friend now wants to make another bet, chances are good that your attitude to the proposition won't be the same as if you had the money. These different reactions introduce another vital point: when we do things with words, we enact not only what we name but also the relationship making the name an act. Language is performative of social being as well as illocutionary force; if words fail to do the things they should, social being has failed as well.

Conversely, whenever language takes, a collectivity affirms *itself* along with its conventional procedures. What holds for the illocutionary minimum of two also holds for the illocutionary mass. Felicitous governmental declarations enact a nation as well as a statute, felicitous baptisms produce communal as well as individual identity.

A scene in Gillo Pontecorvo's film *The Battle of Algiers* (1967) gives memorable expression to the productive power of verbal felicity. Early in the film, which chronicles the Algerian revolution against France's colonial government, an official from the rebellious forces performs a young couple's wedding ceremony and enters their names in a notebook labeled *Algerian Autonomous Zone—Civil Records*. Performance and registration of the marriage are felicitous (and the notebook is a civil record) only in the thought and will of people declared outlaws by established authorities. But the message of the marriage scene is that revolutionary thought and will are overthrowing established authorities in ways besides armed insurrection. Long before there was a free Algeria with its own institutions, Pontecorvo suggests, conventional procedures were making a revolution by producing conventional effects as though free institutions were already in place. The civil records aren't an archive but a notebook, yet collective determination to ignore that self-evident (constative) fact *performed* a real presence in historical time.

To move from the colonies to the homeland, the summer of 1792 was the great divide in the French Revolution, the period when France turned decisively away from its monarchist past and toward its republican future. Early in that summer, on June 26, three months before the republic was proclaimed, the legislature took a measure rich with feeling for the social substance in illocutionary force. By official decree, every commune in France was to erect an "altar of the father-

land" where registration of births, deaths, and marriages would there-
after take place.

Marriages and baptisms are privileged illustrations in speech-act
theory because they unmistakably display the communication of authority from vested institution to performative language. As revolutionary France and Pontecorvo's Algeria understood, the communication is reciprocal. Speech acts performed in the name of the new
mount a powerful insurrection against the sovereignty of the old. Well
before there was a French Republic, speech acts combined with other
kinds to disassemble the French monarchy.

Revolutionary transformations make apparent what can be con-
cealed when societies are stable: performative language not only derives from but also establishes communal reality and institutional
solidity. When a society does things with words, the things and words
affirm it as surely as its conventions bring things and words together.
As a result, a speech-act perspective undoes rigidified concepts of
social history as well as inherited ideas of the referent. The collectivities whose conventions enable performative language are a relational,
dynamic *process* rather than a given, preexistent entity. Like the acts
named by performative verbs, communities and conventions are
within and outside language simultaneously. When words do things,
they actualize their users as well as their meaning.

"This is one way we might justify the 'performative-constative'
distinction—as a distinction between doing and saying" (47). Let's
end this first chapter by giving the "doing" side of Austin's distinction
its due. From Hamlet's "Words words words" to the most recent
iteration of "talk is cheap," language's bad press alludes almost exclusively to words that do nothing more substantive than sound waves'
slight perturbation of the air.

When we felicitously use words to do something, however, substantive action and verbal articulation are one and indivisible. The performative is different because what we say becomes what we live. The
importance of speech-act theory is that doing things with words, like
doing them by other means, can make or unmake our world.

2

Saying Equals Doing

The central point of my first chapter—and a central point of Austin's thought—is that constative and performative language are absolutely distinct. All the effort I devoted to specifying the performative's inter-action with social conventions and production of its own referent had the sole purpose of establishing difference. *How to Do Things with Words* chronicles a discovery, that of the performative. In order to appreciate Austin's achievement, we have to keep constantly in mind that performative language is a separate and unique verbal category.

The central point of this chapter is to contest my first chapter from beginning to end, to show that the constative is in all its features assimilable to the performative. Besides chronicling a discovery, *How to Do Things with Words* ruthlessly and relentlessly challenges what it discovered. In his other essays on speech acts as well as in the Harvard lectures, Austin continually interrogated his most famous concept as soon as he introduced it. The result is a mesmerizing demonstration of how to do things with a mind as well as a seminal description of how to do things with words.

Let's start with what may be the most salient difference between constative and performative, that we evaluate one on the basis of its truth, by asking if it is accurate, and the other on the basis of its felicity, by asking if it works. Even before introducing the concept of the performative, Austin used his first lecture to define the constative as that to which he was *not* devoting attention because it was wholly caught up in the irrelevant problematic of truth and falsity. The descriptive fallacy improvidently sets up reference to objective reality as the only serious affair language undertakes. It condemns students of language to consecrate the entirety of their energy to assessing a verbal statement's validity in relation to a non-verbal situation. Since Austin's purpose was to investigate how verbal statements effect (rather than represent) non-verbal situations, his first move was to exclude representational accuracy from consideration. To analyze

22

how to do things with words, we begin by transcending the "true/false fetish" (151) governing inquiry into how to describe things with words.

Yet the descriptive fallacy had itself come up with apparently constative assertions that went far toward defetishizing the true/false contrast. One of the most famous instances comes from Bertrand Russell's classic 1905 article entitled "On Denoting," which asked how to understand a description when the thing being described doesn't exist. Russell's celebrated example was "The present king of France is bald," and Austin contended that such seemingly constative sentences were in fact not at all subject to the true/false evaluation supposedly applying to all constative descriptions. They were instead instances of the felicitous/infelicitous distinction theoretically restricted to the performative. "The present king of France is bald" goes wrong in the same way as the explicitly performative "I present you the keys to the city" said by someone who doesn't have the keys to present. In both cases, Austin maintains, the sentence is less false than unhappy, and the contrast between constative and performative dematerializes.

> For instance, statements which refer to something which does not exist as, for example, "The present King of France is bald." There might be a temptation to assimilate this to purporting to bequeath something which you do not own. Is there not a presupposition of existence in each? Is not a statement which refers to something which does not exist not so much false as void? And the more we consider a statement not as a sentence (or proposition) but as an act of speech (out of which the others are logical constructions) the more we are studying the whole thing as an act. (20)

Speech acts—performatives—were first contrasted to speech statements, constatives. But the contrast immediately broke down when faulty statements turned out to be faulty for reasons with clear analogies to the factors debilitating failed performatives.

The oppositional breakdown also works the other way. Just as certain constatives seem to be felicitous or infelicitous rather than true or false, certain performatives entail propositional truth in order to do things. If "I present you the keys to the city" is to work, then "I have the keys to the city to present" must state a fact. As Austin put it, "this, it seems clear, commits us to saying that for a certain performative utterance to be happy, certain statements have *to be true*" (45). The performative sentence "I warn you that the bull is about to charge" elicits a famous Austinian interrogative: is my warning felicitous if I know that the bull is actually not going to charge? Whatever answer you give, your constative description of the bull will have impact on your performative speech act of warning, and the dividing line between true/false and felicitous/infelicitous gets thinner and thinner. Austin: "considerations of the happiness and unhappiness type may infect statements (or some statements) and considerations of the type of truth and falsity may infect performatives (or some performatives)" (55).

Imagine yourself promising to do something and then not doing it. Your promise is clearly unhappy, for the conventions of promising require that you keep your word. Now imagine yourself stating that you did something when you haven't done it. You're making a false statement—not to mince words, you're lying—but is your false statement so very different from your false promise? The latter is in the classic form of the explicit performative: first person present-indicative "I promise." The former is an exemplary constative, "I did." Yet it feels awkward to say that the factors invalidating the two utterances are of the true/false species in one case and the felicitous/infelicitous species in the other.

The awkwardness extends even to the sentence Austin often used as the constative at its most straightforward, "The cat is on the mat."

> Suppose I did say "the cat is on the mat" when it is not the case that I believe that the cat is on the mat, what should we say? Clearly it is a case of *insincerity*. In other words: the unhappiness here is, though affecting a statement, exactly the same as the unhappiness infecting "I promise . . ." when I do not intend, do not believe, &c. The insincerity of an assertion is the same as the insincerity of a promise, since both promising and asserting are procedures intended for use by persons having certain thoughts. (50)

A liar's "I promise to send the check tomorrow" and "I sent the check yesterday" are equally invalid even though each is manifestly different in kind from the other. The illocutionary distinction between constative and performative remains pellucid, but in neither case do you get the money.

Categorial collapse has causes besides invalidation of the difference between truth conditions and felicity conditions. Austin also set the performative apart because its referent is within it whereas the constative's referent is outside it. The performative enacts things by saying them, the constative describes things independent of what's said about them. "I bet ten dollars" produces a bet, but "The check's in the mail" does not produce a check.

Still, "I assert that the check's in the mail" *does* produce an assertion, as "I state that I already paid you" makes a statement. Everything that speech-act theory has discovered about explicit first-person performatives—*I bet, I warn, I promise, I solemnly swear, I hereby declare,* and a host of others—applies directly to any constative utterance preceded by a formula equivalent to "I say that." Although he fretted over the "apparent danger" of turning all utterances into performatives, Austin was well aware that the identity of speaking and doing was true of " 'I state that' (to utter which *is* to state) as well as 'I bet that.' In both examples there is the same asymmetry between first person and other uses" (65). This asymmetry exists because words always do what they state when the speaker says that he or she is stating. Like "I do" at a wedding, "I say" in any circumstances establishes a perfect congruence between words and their referent.

When I first read Austin seriously, I was unimpressed by this part of his argument. As I believe is true of most people, I was attracted to speech-act theory because the overt performative, by simultaneously creating a thing and activating a social convention, overturns the word/thing and language/society oppositions I found intuitively wrong even though broadly accepted. But "I state" and "I assert" struck me as different in kind from "I apologize" and "I promise." Austin seemed to be playing with words here; "I state that the constitution is suspended" and "I declare that the constitution is suspended" may be verbally similar, but for me the declaration performed an act of incomparably more interest than the statement.

I'm now convinced and excited by what I used to think unconvincing and unexciting. The fact made obvious by the performative, that the illocutionary force borne by words is always also a relationship lived by people, applies less obviously but just as importantly to the constative, and the "I say" model helps show why. What we say is very much part of our relationships when they're shaky, as we often make explicit; "They say cut back, we say fight back" is unfortunately a much-chanted slogan at my university. While "cut back" and "fight back" don't qualify as simple assertions of fact, many other uses of conflictual "say" do, as in the famous cartoon caption "I still say it's spinach and I say the hell with it!" Or take a parent's "You *say* you did your homework" or a neighbor's "You *say* your dog never left your yard" or a spouse's "You *say* you don't have time to come with me" (all emphasis in original).

Since we explicitly perform what we "say" as a speech act when we disagree, saying things must also be active when we agree; if statements perform conflict, they also perform concord. To assert together—"We have been born again"; "The Führer is always right"; "God gave this land to us"; "Reagan understands what it means to make a payroll"—does something quite real. Identifying (explicit or implicit) "I state" and "we assert" as performative is, despite my original misapprehension, an excellent means of suggesting why statements are also performances.

"Did you say the king's in the counting house, counting out his money? I bet ten dollars the queen's in the parlor, eating bread and honey." Each of those sentences contains a proposition about objective reality, where the king and queen are and what they're doing. Each introduces the reference to reality with what is in the generalized sense a performative verb, "bet" and "say." In both cases, speech-act theory directs attention *away from* objective reality and *toward* the social relationship that makes the verb felicitous. Whether we say something or bet something, we're involved in a conventional procedure as independent of what we say as of how much we bet.

Regardless of what you think about implicit "I state," however, the performative/constative opposition still can't last. Even banal everyday phrases like "I'm sorry" throw it into disarray. Is "I'm sorry" a constative description of feelings like "I'm sad"? Or is it a performative apology, a paraphrase of the explicit first-person speech act "I apologize"? "I'm sorry" certainly appears in many circumstances where it's equivalent to "I apologize." On the other hand, dialogues like "I'm sorry" "Oh no you're not" show that the words continue to bear constative content as well as constative form. Like all performatives, "I apologize" can't be false: to say that you apologize is in and of itself to make an apology. But to say "I'm sorry" is also to make an apology even though those words purport to describe and can therefore be assessed as accurate or inaccurate. Most of us can remember our parents forcing us to say we were sorry for something we weren't in the least sorry about, and both our parents' insistence and our own reluctance demonstrate the performative power of constative language with no truth value at all. How can constative and performative be separate kinds of language when the same words belong on both sides of the dividing line without really fitting in either place?

Austin continually lamented his failure to maintain the characteristics he put forward to differentiate constative from performative. This confession of failure begins Lecture VI: "even a list of all possible criteria [...] certainly would not distinguish performatives from constatives, as very commonly the *same* sentence is used on different occasions of utterance in *both* ways, performative and constative. The thing seems hopeless from the start" (67). Although Lecture VII tones down the hopelessness for a more sedate rhetoric, the situation remains just what it was in Lecture VI.

Now let us consider where we stand for a moment: beginning with the supposed contrast between performative and constative utterances, we found sufficient indications that unhappiness nevertheless seems to characterize both kinds of utterance, not merely the performative; and that the requirement of conforming or bearing some relation to the facts, different in different cases, seems to characterize performatives, in addition to the requirement that they should be happy, similarly to the way which is characteristic of supposed constatives. (91)

While that passage prefaces announcement of a "fresh start on the problem" (91), the fresh start comes to a stale conclusion. From whatever perspective we contemplate it, the performative/constative opposition raises as many problems as it solves.

The primary reason for the problems raised is fundamentally the same as the reason for the problems solved: when speech-act theory contextualizes utterances by directing attention to the things they do as *illocutions*, it simultaneously makes it impossible to decontextualize utterances by attending solely to what they say as *locutions*. The fallacious component of the descriptive fallacy is not only that it ignores the great spectrum of performatives that do things other than describe. Just as importantly, exclusive concentration on a description's coefficient of accuracy obliterates all the things descriptions themselves do. The capital difference between locutionary status and illocutionary force—between speech and speech acts, between words' meaning and their effect—by no means functions solely in overt performatives. A descriptive utterance has in many cases overpowering impact on the situation in which it's made.

An easy way to feel the extent to which this is so is to imagine a state of affairs that includes a condition embarrassing to one of the people involved. Say John has a large piece of bright green vegetable matter stuck between his front teeth while you, John, and a group of comparative strangers whom John wants to impress are discussing the federal budget deficit. If you interrupt the discussion to announce what you see to John and the others present, you have provided a description meeting all possible criteria of truth and accuracy. But it would be fallacious beyond belief to pretend that providing a description was the only thing you had done. Saying what is can affect a set of circumstances with every bit of the dynamically transformational impact that Austin first invoked to show that words do things other than say what is.

Let's keep picking on John. Now his teeth are flawless, and he's discussing the budget deficit with eloquence, verve, and thoroughly convincing logic. So you state (truly) that John wears elevator shoes and still comes up only to the shoulder of a man of average height. Again the rigorous accuracy of your description hardly counts, for again you have used words to do things other than describe even though there's absolutely nothing except a true description in all the words you used. An utterance's locutionary definition is no less incomplete when words describe than when they act.

Or say your comment to John is the admiring but quite sincere "You're speaking with eloquence, verve, and thoroughly convincing logic." While truth is once more respected as it should be, it's again obviously fallacious to maintain that the only, or even the principal, function of your statement is to describe. Like an insult, a compliment has precise and powerful illocutionary force even when its linguistic form and its truth value satisfy all the criteria identifying the constative.

In general, the propositional content of a constative sentence is indeed easier to separate from the circumstances of utterances than that of an overt performative. But this ease of separation doesn't make the act of separation more legitimate. When we state something, it's rare indeed for us to have no effect beyond producing the statement, and to understand the effect we have we must look past and around the statement's propositional content.

As Austin put it while contemplating the baldness of the present king of France, "the more we consider a statement not as a sentence (or proposition) but as an act of speech (out of which the others are logical constructions) the more we are studying the whole thing as an act" (20). The key opposition isn't between constative statements and performative acts but between constative acts and the "logical constructions" that can be made from them by ignoring the act performed and addressing only the "proposition" contained in the "sentence." It is of course feasible to evaluate propositions about the green thing between John's teeth without referring at all to those propositions' effect on their hearers and speakers. But why would anyone want to?

To look at statements and see "the whole thing as an act" is to recognize that the whole thing, the statement and the act, cannot without great loss be isolated one from the other: "we have been realizing more and more clearly that the occasion of an utterance matters seriously, and that the words used are to some extent to be 'explained' by the 'context' in which they are designed to be or have actually been spoken in a linguistic interchange" (100). The statement that John wears elevator shoes is as a logical and descriptive proposition, as a locution, everywhere and always identical to itself. But as an illocutionary act, it varies stunningly as the occasion of utterance shifts from a whisper in a friend's ear to the opening line of your formal introduction of John before his speech to a large audience.

With constative as with performative, therefore, the imperative is always to contextualize, and once again constative and performative collapse into one another.

> In order to explain what can go wrong with statements we cannot just concentrate on the proposition involved (whatever that is) as has been done traditionally. We must consider the total situation in which the utterance is issued—the total speech-act—if we are to see the parallel between statements and performative utterances, and how each can go wrong. So the total speech act in the total speech situation is emerging from logic piecemeal as important in special cases: and thus we are assimilating the supposed constative utterance to the performative. (52)

Austin's development of the last sentence in that passage is crucial. The importance of "the total speech act in the total speech situation" entails "assimilating the supposed constative utterance to the performative." Envisioning language as a component of human interaction led Austin to discover the performative. That same vision led him to see that he was wrong to distinguish the performative from what is now no more than the "supposed constative."

It's worth pausing here to go back over the steps by which Austin's situational and socialized perspective led to diametrically opposed definitions of the performative/constative couple. Step One is dissatisfaction with the way the descriptive fallacy takes words away from their speakers. We don't use language simply to describe; we also use it to act, and in order to see its executive power we must look at the ways it transforms the situations in which it occurs. When a marriage takes place, when a bet is made, when war is declared, when warning is given, the world is not the same as it was before. To compare words and the world as if each were static and frozen is inane when the point of moment is their dynamically reciprocal effects on one another.

Attention to the conditions under which speech acts does far more than highlight the special quality of the performative. It also reveals that the constative has comparably vigorous impact, that it too is in dynamic interaction with those who use it and with the protocols governing their relationship. For the performative, Rule A.1 establishes the foundational condition for words' active capacity, the existence of a certain conventional procedure with conventional effect. But conventional procedures are equally functional when the constative is at issue. Austin emphasized that point by articulating it in conjunction with one of the few exclamation points in *How to Do Things with Words*: "a parallel presupposition to A.1 exists with statements also!" (51).

To appreciate the extent to which this is so, list some of those to whom you could comfortably say that they have a piece of spinach stuck between their teeth—a spouse, a friend, a child, and so forth. Now list some of those to whom you could not comfortably say the same thing—a judge, a bum, a policeman, a stranger on the street. The conventions aren't nearly so strict as those governing a structured performative ceremony like marriage, but it's obviously incorrect to say that convention counts in one case but not in the other. The difference is of degree rather than kind, and the same is true of all the other rules supposedly demarcating the performative from its constative other. That a statement is true in no way implies that it can be made without regard for the relationship between its speaker and hearers.

Toward the end of the Harvard lectures, Austin's remorseless interrogation of the performative/constative distinction led him to suggest that there might nevertheless be relatively pure examples that could be legitimately and unapologetically opposed. Two of his instances were "I apologize" for the performative and his old favorite "The cat is on the mat" for the constative. "I apologize" is indeed very close to a pure performative, one for which *all* that counts is a convention and the words enacting it. Regardless of how you feel or what you think, when you say "I apologize" you've made your apology in due and proper form. Analogously, "The cat is on the mat" seems to approach the sheerly constative status of a proposition in which all that matters is the information conveyed.

Yet even "The cat is on the mat" does things other than describe. While it's certainly the most frequent proposition in *How to Do Things with Words*, in none of its multiple occurrences there does it convey any information whatever about a cat or a mat. Moreover, even if we accord it full descriptive accuracy, an instant's reflection is enough to see that we wouldn't normally say it *simply* to describe. You would say "The cat is on the mat" when appropriate not only to the position of the cat but also to your relationship with the person to whom you're speaking. If a friend is looking for the cat, aren't you more likely to say where it is than when an enemy wants it? If someone needs the mat to take a sunbath, doesn't your relationship to the person determine whether you decide that the cat's comfort is more important? If you've just been reading Dr. Seuss's *The Cat in the Hat* to a child, doesn't the sight of a cat on a mat give you and the child more of an opportunity to continue Seuss-speak than to convey information to one another?

This is another case where hypothetical situations could be extended at will, and again the point is not the quantity of situations that can be imagined but the daunting difficulty of coming up with a situation in which to *say* "The cat is on the mat" is not also to *do* something with, to, for, despite, or against someone else at the same time. The coordinates of the cat's location are only one of a great many components determining the words we use to say where it is, and an Austinian perspective on language makes it impossible to privilege one of those components over the others. The minimal constative utterance "The cat is on the mat" can have a vast range of performative impact.

Drop Austin's example and come up with your own. Remember the last purely constative sentence you spoke before starting to read. In my case, the last statement of naked fact I made before coming to write was "You woke me up," and both I and the person to whom I was talking were well aware that stating a fact was in no way the main thing I was doing. It's often the case that such lapidary constatives without rhetorical flourishes—"She started it"; "I love you"; "That's your fourth beer"—are more intensely active than utterances that would seem to be striving for higher performative density. Proverbially, the truth hurts. Actually, it does countless other things as well. In almost no case is its sole function to give verbal form to a non-verbal reality. Austin's conclusion: "Once we realize that what we have to study is *not* the sentence but the issuing of an utterance in a speech situation, there can hardly be any longer a possibility of not seeing that stating is performing an act" (139).

Austin's originary opposition between constative and performative was that between saying and doing, with the corollary opposition between the truth value of the constative and the productive efficacy of the performative. As he explored his insights into the ways saying and doing are interconnected, therefore, he was also breaking down the opposition between truth value and productive efficacy. The breakdown reaches its most acute stage in Lecture XI, the next-to-last chapter in *How to Do Things with Words*. There Austin not only shows that expressing truth is far from the sole function of a successful constative proposition. He goes much farther and examines the possibility that truth itself is a conventional construct displaying the same social variability as the procedures underlying canonical speech acts like making a bet or a promise. The question asked by Lecture XI is this: Can the constative's truth value be itself a performance subject to collective protocols with the same *constitutive* power as those establishing every other illocutionary force?

The starting point for the question is yet another summary of why the performative/constative contrast melts under scrutiny.

> Discussion of doing and saying certainly seems to point to the conclusion that whenever I "say" anything (except perhaps a mere exclama-

tion like "damn" or "ouch") I shall be performing both locutionary
and illocutionary acts, and these two kinds of acts seem to be the
very things which we tried to use, under the names of "doing" and
"saying," as a means of distinguishing performatives from constatives. If we are in general always doing both things, how can our
distinction survive? (133)

The concluding question is not quite entirely rhetorical, but it comes
very close.

A locution states, an illocution performs: but when we look at the
conditions under which statements are actually produced, we immediately see that they too are putting on performances. "Surely to state
is every bit as much to perform an illocutionary act as, say, to warn
or to pronounce. [. . .] 'Stating' seems to meet all the criteria we had
for distinguishing the illocutionary act" (134). When we tell the truth,
we do so many other things at the same time that it's foolish to
venerate the truth told as if it alone were consequential.

Lecture XI makes its points about saying and stating the truth in
several ways before broaching the problem of *what* is stated. When
Austin directly confronts the truth, however, he sees exactly the same
difficulty presented by the statement. We tend to consider both
terms—*truth* and *statement*—as though they designated absolute realities when they actually vary with circumstances. As a statement
cannot be abstracted from those who make it, so the truth cannot be
dissociated from those who believe it.

> Is the constative, then, always true or false? When a constative is
> confronted with the facts, we in fact appraise it in ways involving
> the employment of a vast array of terms which overlap with those
> that we use in the appraisal of performatives. In real life, as opposed
> to the simple situations envisaged in logical theory, one cannot al-
> ways answer in a simple manner whether it is true or false. (142–
> 43)

Real life is social life, complexly social life. Its contrast to the "simple
situations envisaged in logical theory" is identical to that earlier established between the "act of speech" and the "sentence" or "proposition"
that are "logical constructions" out of that act (20). In each case, logic
fabricates an abstraction that philosophers can treat in contented
disregard for the human environment it comes from. The vision of the
world producing speech-act theory moved inexorably toward contex-
tualizing the truth language communicates as well as the medium of
communication.

How do you contextualize truth? Austin gives several examples,
the first being a cliché of geography, "France is hexagonal." That

geometric equivalency comes from the fact that France's borders comprise six major geographic features, the Alps, the Pyrenees, the Mediterranean, the Atlantic, and so on. It's so standard a description that the French often refer to their homeland as "the hexagon," and the idea of the six-sided nation is among the first characterizations presented to students of French history and culture.

That France is hexagonal may be broadly repeated, but is it true? Austin says that we can't answer this question without defining the conditions under which the answer is to circulate. For people concerned with the purity of geometric figures, it's arrant nonsense to say that France has anything in common with a hexagon. For people concerned with acquiring a general sense of France's borders, hexagonal language is quite satisfactory. Though it would be hard to find a statement simpler than the three words "France is hexagonal," this straightforward form produces a highly complex problem of content. While statements are supposed to be either true or false, they're often neither one nor the other. " 'France is hexagonal' [. . .] is a rough description. It is not a true or a false one" (143). The "supposed constative" (52, 91) is a hypothetical entity in part because the truth it supposedly conveys is itself subject to conventional determination.

Austin's second non-true and non-false constative is "Lord Raglan won the battle of Alma," a fact of British history for which a satisfactory American equivalent is "General Meade won the battle of Gettysburg." Since soldiers rather than generals fight battles, is it true or false to say that generals rather than soldiers win them? Again the answer depends on the situation, for there are circumstances in which such statements are right and circumstances in which they are wrong. Because "the intents and purposes of the utterance and its context are important" (143), we cannot enshrine truth as all-important and judge every utterance on the basis of its accuracy. Like France's hexagonal shape, Lord Raglan's great victory is "suitable to some contexts and not to others; it would be pointless to insist on its truth or falsity" (144). At least its truth or falsity in the abstract: in order to insist on one or the other, we must first know the conventions governing truth and falsity in the concrete conditions before us.

Austin's many iterations of the speech-act vision of truth all emphasize that the death of the constative/performative opposition is the birth of the opposition between language in itself and language in the world, between locutions and illocutions. We cannot say what's true until we know the conventions applying where and when truth is being expressed.

It is essential to realize that "true" and "false," like "free" and "unfree," do not stand for anything simple at all; but only for a general dimen-

> sion of being a right or proper thing to say as opposed to a wrong
> thing, in these circumstances, to this audience, for these purposes
> and with these intentions [. . .] The truth or falsity of a statement
> depends not merely on the meanings of words but on what act you
> were performing in what circumstances.
>
> What then finally is left of the distinction of the performative and
> constative utterance? (145)

Once more the question isn't entirely rhetorical, but once more it
comes awfully close. While it remains possible to abstract utterances
from their human context in such a way that the constative stands in
pristine opposition to the performative, this abstraction does bloody
violence to all the features that make the performative interesting in
the first place. To see the constative in action rather than in thought
is to see that both it and the truth it conveys are as much a part of
collective exchange as the most immediately consequential performative: "the traditional 'statement' is an abstraction, an ideal, and so is
its traditional truth or falsity" (148). Although abstractions and ideals
are always lovely to contemplate, their enticing clarity in no way
privileges them over the messily concrete social situations that are
speech-act theory's special sphere. While we can state truth in such a
way that it appears always and everywhere true, to do so we must
ignore all the dimensions of human existence that make truth worth
knowing.

> Truth and falsity are (except by an artificial abstraction which is
> always possible and legitimate for certain purposes) not names for
> relations, qualities, or what not, but for a dimension of assessment—
> how the words stand in respect of satisfactoriness to the facts, events,
> situation, &c., to which they refer. (149)

Not a quality but an assessment—identical to the felicity conditions
of the performative, the truth conditions of the constative are in each
fiber of their being interwoven with the members of a human
collectivity. To state the truth is not only to do other things besides.
It is also to accept the criteria of truth set up and defended by systemic
social protocols. Far more than an adjunct to its informational content, the performative character of the constative is inherent in the
information itself.

That is why it's of the first importance for Austin to insist that the
concept of illocution applies to the constative no less than to the
performative: "stating is only one among very numerous speech acts of
the illocutionary class" (147). As society and its conventions absolutely
determine when we get married and make a bet, so they have decisive

impact on when we tell the truth and tell a lie. Because "the illocutionary act is a conventional act: an act done as conforming to a convention" (105), unequivocally stipulating that the constative is an illocution makes what the constative expresses conventional as well. Although we may well continue to see the constative as either true or false and the performative as either felicitous or infelicitous, we must go through a community to understand which words are true no less than to understand which words do things.

Language both states and performs. Its ability to do *both* comes from the society in which it communicates. "Stating, describing, &c., are *just two* names among a very great many others for illocutionary acts; they have no unique position" (148–49). Truth too is a verbal performance that succeeds or fails according to the stance adopted toward it by a specific collectivity. It too is happy or unhappy not in and of itself but in function of those among whom it hits or misses.

When Austin incorporates statements of truth among "a very great many other" illocutionary acts while insisting on illocution's ineluctable conventionality, he displays clear affinities with several contemporary continental philosophers who have also explored the ways society constitutes its facts. Figures like Michel Foucault, Roland Barthes, and all those who have developed the thought of Friedrich Nietzsche have made the conventional nature of truth a fundamental principle. The entire post-structuralist tradition has illuminated facets of truth that could readily serve as demonstrative material for *How to Do Things with Words*. The large corpus of recent research into the strength of ideology in everyday life is also pertinent, for ideology's capacity to constitute its own validation is among the most striking examples of how a collectivity does things with words.

These connections between the Anglo-American tradition of speech-act theory and the European tradition of structuralist and post-structuralist orientation are both real and significant; they have made no small contribution to spreading Austin's influence among literary critics, as this book's next section will consider in detail. Nevertheless, there are crucial points at which Austin's affinities with continental thought disappear. The areas of intersection are by no means universal.

Austin declines to participate in the comprehensive ontological assertions that sometimes characterize continental philosophy's inquiry into the empire of symbolic form. His concern is not to repudiate all possibility of according truth its traditional august independence but to show why that independence is irrelevant to the status of truth as a functioning agent of social coexistence. Austin often interrupts his representations of statements as concrete communal performances to remind us that they also exist as ideal abstractions "always possible and legitimate for certain purposes" (149). The decision not to address the status of truth outside society doesn't in his case involve a concomitant conviction that truth is nowhere else to be found. The objection to assigning truth or falsity to "France is hexagonal" in no way derived from uncertainty about whether France and hexagons are real. Austin's argument was rather that reality isn't in play, that we judge statements not by comparing them to what they represent but by assessing their adequacy to a social function.

Even during his pointed repudiation of fetishized truth in Lecture XI, Austin contends that truth value can legitimately become our principal concern if we abstract a constative description from those who make and receive it.

> With the constative utterance, we abstract from the illocutionary (let alone the perlocutionary) aspects of the speech act, and we concentrate on the locutionary: moreover, we use an over-simplified notion of correspondence with the facts—over-simplified because essentially it brings in the illocutionary aspect. This is the ideal of what would be right to say in all circumstances, for any purpose, to any audience, &c. Perhaps it is sometimes realized. (145–46)

As a locution, the constative can be taken as simply presenting some degree of "correspondence with the facts." But every constative actually produced "brings in the illocutionary act": irrespective of its success or failure in corresponding to the facts, it *also* performs an interaction between people. Although the ideal of an utterance appropriate to all people in all circumstances may "sometimes" be realized, this ideal has nothing to do with the force of speech acts constituted through the conventions observed by speakers at a certain time and place.

The locution/illocution contrast, which distinguishes the object of inquiry addressed by formal linguistics from that of speech-act theory, also distinguishes the *referential* concerns of the descriptive fallacy from Austin's *social* project. If we remove an utterance from the circumstances of its production, then linguistic form and descriptive value constitute its sole identity. But when we refuse such an "oversimplified notion" of linguistic identity and place utterances in context, the illocutionary conventions of Rule A.1 immediately reestablish their primacy. The constative's *illocutionary* force is always distinct from its descriptive accuracy.

But at the same time, the constative's illocutionary force constitutes a substantial collective presence, which introduces another capital difference between Austin and recent continental philosophers. For speech-act theory, representational statements can never be understood as the free play of liberated language simply because they fail to provide a reliable representation of objective reality. Despite that failure, they nevertheless perform social reality as validated by the members of a given collectivity. There is a double sense in which stating and describing "have no unique position" (149) among speech acts. Just as important as their subordination to the conventions governing all other illocutions is the fact that statements, like all other illocutions, bear great responsibilities for maintaining the communities in which they circulate.

Conventional fabrication of constative truth doesn't prevent statements performed as valid from affecting lives with all truth's traditional might. Austin's insight that things can be done by words never slips over into the suggestion that the things done are somehow unreal. The constative has special status among illocutions neither in its origin nor in its repercussion. It too comes from collective protocols, it too has capital influence on collective life.

When you think about it, it's curious that the performative/constative opposition has continued to thrive even though the man who introduced it exuberantly repudiated it. My decision to write the first chapter of this book as though the opposition were unproblematic is congruent with the practice of many other devotees of speech-act theory, who often join Austin himself in starkly contrasting constative and performative before detailing the many reasons for assimilating them. I believe that the reason for this continued life of an aborted opposition is that it offers a handy way to preserve respect for constative truth, to ward off the sensation that words are nothing but words when they are actually among our most substantial collective realities. It's not enough to recognize that the facts conveyed by a verbal statement are identical in kind to the conventions activated by a verbal performance. We must also be aware that these facts nevertheless figure among the dominant constituents of collective being. Simultaneous affirmation of the performative/constative identity *and* the performative/constative opposition gives the constative its due without misrepresenting its nature.

The fable of the Emperor's new clothes can help specify the distance between the constative and the referential while also showing the power words wield in communities. So long as his subjects refuse to say that the Emperor is naked for fear of appearing to lack the virtue required to see his clothes, the referential fact of his nudity is collectively non-existent. Life goes on as if the Emperor were majestically attired; all the conventions of his reign are observed and respected.

His clothes are *performed* by a community willing to speak and act as if he were actually wearing them.

Moreover, when the little child says "But he has nothing on!" and the citizenry uproariously concurs, the fable doesn't simply represent a population's progress from illusion to reality. It shows the Emperor's nudity being *performed* just like his clothes, by utterance of a statement communally affirmed as the truth. In one sense, the "ideal" sense that comes from "an oversimplified notion of correspondence with the facts," the child's exclamation is the straight truth and the wicked tailors' spiel a straight lie. Yet the fable has so much appeal because the straight facts aren't operative. The Emperor's referential condition is exactly the same before and after the child's exclamation, but his constative identity has changed beyond endurance. The words "But he has nothing on!" did something momentous, and it won't do to assign the source of their power solely to the facts; before the words, the facts were the same as afterwards.

What changes in the course of the story? Not the Emperor's objective condition but communal statement of it. "He's wearing clothes the impure cannot see" becomes "he's not wearing anything at all," and there is no story—no narrative, no transformation—unless that verbal shift occurs. Referentially, the Emperor is naked at the beginning of his walk among his subjects and naked at the end of it. Constatively, he loses his clothes as the walk progresses. Although we can always abstract the Emperor from his society and see him as he really is, to do so misses the point entirely.

Games display the nature of constative truth with particular clarity, which is why speech-act theorists get such mileage from them. While Austin's favorite game allusion was to cricket, baseball is a comparably fertile source. In addition to specifying what counts as a ball or a strike, for instance, the rules of baseball give the umpire the exclusive right to determine whether those conditions have been met. There's an old and probably apocryphal story about an umpire's exercise of this right that sounds as if his preferred book were *How to Do Things with Words*. A pitch comes in, the umpire's call is delayed, the batter yells "It's a ball," the catcher yells "It's a strike," and the umpire settles the argument by calmly announcing that "It ain't nothing till I say so."

In that situation, there is of course a referential fact about where the pitch went and whether the rules define its trajectory as a ball or a strike. But that referential fact ain't nothing. All that counts is the umpire's constative speech act of *saying* "Strike!" or "Ball!" Like the Emperor's nakedness, the pitch's position is inoperative until language performs it.

In *The Structure of Scientific Revolutions*, T. S. Kuhn describes a psychological experiment relevant to the Austinian constative. The subjects of the experiment were to identify playing cards presented to them for brief periods of time, and among the cards were some in which the colors were reversed: hearts and diamonds were black, spades and clubs red. When the miscolored cards appeared for extremely short periods, they were regularly identified as one of the normal suits; subjects might call a black heart a heart or a club, but they didn't perceive it as in any way anomalous. As the time of exposure increased, the subjects' confidence decreased. They first recognized that something was wrong without being able to say what and then, as the cards appeared for longer and longer intervals, finally saw the disparity between shape and color.

In this validation of the old philosophical principle that there are no percepts without concepts, the subjects' originally confident (mis)-statements can also be taken to show why the constative and the referential cannot be identified. Again, an objective fact fails to achieve discursive presence, again discourse continues irrespective of its descriptive failure, and again abstracting the referent from human representation misses the point altogether. For the subjects involved, playing cards' anomalies don't matter so long as articulation of their identities proceeds undisturbed.

My reason for discussing contradictions between constative and referential truth is not at all to maintain that the constative is never objectively accurate. The idea is rather that objective accuracy is immaterial to the constative's social power, and that disjunction is far more apparent when social power accompanies objective error. Even when constative and referential coincide perfectly, moreover, it's not this coincidence that makes truth felicitous. The decisive factor is still a collectivity's stance. Once the constative is assimilated to the performative, truth value joins felicity conditions among conventional procedures. When there is no possible doubt that the umpire's call faithfully represents the pitch's trajectory, it remains the call rather than the trajectory that counts.

Take two new Ph.D.'s beginning their academic careers. One is brilliant, the other sub-mediocre. But many people say that the sub-mediocre intellect is brilliant, no one says the brilliant intellect is better than mediocre. Which receives the better job offer?

Or imagine two candidates for political office, one with the moral and mental capacity to become a statesman for the ages, the other a mental and moral vacuum with seductively telegenic features. When more people constatively assert a positive assessment of the telegenic nonentity, their performative act of voting will proceed accordingly.

We can of course reverse these two scenarios and bring constative representation and objective truth into conformity. Now the brilliant Ph.D. is called what she is, the potentially great statesman enjoys a more seemly discursive identity. The radical change of probable careers is nonetheless due not to inherent qualities but to the way identity is verbally performed in social discourse. As Austin said, what counts in constative truth is not a quality but an assessment; focusing on qualities in themselves muddies the waters.

Like every other exchange of commodities, the art market arrestingly displays the social performance of constative truth. How much is a painting worth? What people are willing to pay for it. How much are they willing to pay for it? What people say it's worth. A commodity is defined by the primacy of exchange value over use value. Exchange value is constative, use value referential, and every aspect of existence in a society where commodities circulate offers instances of the constative tearing the referential apart.

Since the way to define the referential use value of a painting isn't readily apparent, consider constative representation in the stock market. There are huge numbers of objective indices for the monetary value of a given company's stock, indices like the ratio of assets to obligations or stock price to corporate earnings. Even though such statistics quantify a company's financial condition with unexceptionable objectivity, a glance at any newspaper's financial pages shows that the (constative) price of stocks presents a huge range of relations to corporations' (referential) value. The stock of a healthy company that everybody says is sick goes down; that of a sick company that everybody says is healthy goes up. A killing in the market is an especially lucrative example of the things done with words.

Say there *is* some infallibly revelatory fact about a corporation that strictly determines the price of its stock. Although the financial pages become much less interesting, they still show the performative nature of constative truth for the simple reason that the great revelatory fact operates not in a vacuum but in society. Stock prices would in this hypothetical scenario remain the consequence of human decisions despite the fact that those decisions are reached on the basis of a mechanical algorithm. As they are, stock markets are speech-act laboratories because they present so vast a range of relations between constative and referential value. If you reduce that range to a single invariable ratio, you conceal the power of speech acts without in any way reducing it. Regardless of whether collective statements conform to or diverge from objective facts, the statements maintain determinant influence on collective behavior. And collective behavior, not objective facts, makes a stock rise and fall in price.

The money gained or lost in the stock market loses none of its purchasing power because it has so shifty a referential ground. Analogously, the social authority of other kinds of constative assessments can display great strength regardless of their basis in fact. The truth that is the conventional effect of conventional procedures, while it may inspire less awe than truth in itself, is not a bit less functional. Statements of fact circulating through a community do things quite unattributable to the actual existence of the fact stated.

As with the performative, therefore, the paramount demand for understanding the constative is to look first at the community where language is felicitous. Whether saying or doing things, words always also enact their speakers. Some years ago, a collection of logical problems like the farmer crossing the river with a fox, a goose, and a sack of grain included this: A surgeon and his son were in an automobile accident that killed the surgeon instantly. When the severely injured son was brought to the hospital, the surgeon took one look and screamed, "My God! It's my son!" How is this possible?

The surgeon at the hospital was of course the boy's mother, and it's likely that equal opportunity in medical schools has made this puzzler no longer puzzling. If so, its present transparency is as bound up with collective conventions as its former opacity. The presence and absence of gender specification in a constative "surgeon" are equally expressive (and performative) of communal reality. Words say what we are as well as performing us, and speech-act theory addresses both these components of language's comprehensively socialized identity.

I ended the first chapter by celebrating the power of the performative while contrasting it to the constative. Since this chapter makes the contrast untenable, it also makes the celebration unrestricted. Austin's insight into the force of words given currency by social conventions applies to verbal statements as well as verbal identity. The constative too is a performance that can have life-transforming or life-arresting effects on its audience and its referent.

3

Saying, Doing, and Writing

Despite their double position on the constative/performative relationship, my first two chapters actually have a single focus; both explore Austinian concentration on human interaction in and through language, on linguistic action in and through society. Putting speech and speakers together first leads to isolating the performative and then ends its isolation. The locution/illocution distinction survives because it contrasts language in society to language in the abstract; the constative/performative distinction dies because both its terms encompass language and society at once. Identifying the constative as a performative proclaims language's social identity perhaps even more spectacularly than discovering the performative in the first place.

Austin's commentators have assumed hugely different stances toward the performative/constative contrast/identity, stances that seem to be connected with the commentator's disciplinary formation. Some students of speech-act theory have been aghast that the theory's founder thoroughly undermined the opposition on which his theory was constructed; others have voiced their delight at so exemplary a refusal to pay obeisance to categorial orderliness. Whereas literary critics figure prominently among those who find real pleasure in following Austin all the way, linguists have tended to wish rather that he hadn't gone so far.

Part of the reason for linguists' hesitation is undoubtedly that the axioms of their discipline's principal branches rigorously prohibit the socialized understanding responsible for collapsing the constative into the performative. Those for whom language is independent of the configuration of any given collectivity understandably have strong reservations about Austin's ability to put the linguistic and collective together. Speech-act theory offers a challenging, powerful alternative to formalist linguistics, and one important response to the challenge has been an attempt to redefine the performative as simultaneously out of touch with the constative and out of reach of society. The two most powerful contemporary schools of formal linguistics, Saussurean structuralism and Chomskyan transformational grammar, have each produced a well-known effort to keep constative and performative reliably distinct.

For good reason, Emile Benveniste is internationally recognized as one of those who brought structural linguistics to the forefront of research in the humanities and social sciences. The essays collected in the two volumes of Benveniste's *Problems of General Linguistics* have been citations of choice in a variety of scholarly fields, for Benveniste has an admirable ability to illuminate language while simultaneously opening fruitful paths of research for disciplines other than linguistics. Given the great importance structuralism has had in literary studies, Benveniste's reaction to Austin in the essay called "Analytical Philosophy and Language" is of special interest here.

After acknowledging the linguistic significance of the performative/constative opposition, Benveniste contends that it deserves protection from the second thoughts of the man who introduced it. Because Austin can't have been "right to set up a distinction and then immediately go about watering it down and weakening it to the point of making one doubt its existence" (Benveniste 1971; p. 234), Benveniste sets out to resolidify the dividing line.

To do so, he establishes a stringent qualification for both the linguistic and social components of the interaction between language and society that is performative speech. Linguistically, Benveniste says that "performative utterances are those in which a declarative-jussive verb in the first person of the present is constructed with a dictum" (234–235). His example is a head of state's *I order that the population be mobilized*, which shares the structure of other explicit declarative-jussive utterances like *I swear that . .* , *I promise to . . .* and *I renounce. . . .* In all cases, the key criterion is that the verb be jussive as well as declarative. Verbs that are merely declarative can't qualify. *I say that the store is closed*, for example, is declarative but not jussive and is as a consequence constative not performative. While such statements of fact display surface resemblances to *I order that the population be mobilized*, they state the case without in any way altering it. When, in Benveniste's terminology, we have a factum—*the store is closed*—rather than a dictum—*the population is to be mobilized*—we don't have a speech act.

Even speech that seems to act is for Benveniste not performative if it fails to display the proper linguistic form, for we must always seek "a more and more vivid awareness of the formal specificity of linguistic facts" (231). Austin argued that imperative verbs have obvious performative force because we're doing the same thing with words when we say *Come here* as when we use the first-person declarative-jussive *I order you to come here.* For Benveniste, however, every performative utterance must be verbalized in a single way: "the linguistic form must conform to a specific model, that of the verb in the present and in the first person [. . .] It can thus be seen that an imperative is not the equivalent of a performative utterance by reason of the fact that it is neither an utterance nor performative" (237). Analogously, despite Austin's opinion, a sign on a junkyard fence reading "Guard Dogs" doesn't constitute the performative act of warning. "Only the formula, 'I warn you that,' assuming that it has been produced by someone in authority, is a performative notice" (238). The watchword is that of a structuralist critic before a literary text: look at the language and nothing else. While Austin's performative incorporates utterances regardless of form, Benveniste's requires an invariable formal model.

And where Austin saw social conventions pervading language, Benveniste limits them to those operative when a performative manifests hierarchical distinctions of superiority and inferiority. The curious parenthetical remark in the previous quotation, Benveniste's suggestion that I'm unable to warn you of anything unless I'm "someone in authority," is congruent with a general conviction that performative speech always manifests a social pecking order. This conviction is very strong indeed.

> In any case, a performative utterance has no reality except as it is authenticated as an *act.* Outside the circumstances that make it performative, such an utterance is nothing at all. Anybody can shout in the public square, "I decree a general mobilization," and as it cannot be an *act* because the requisite authority is lacking, such an utterance is no more than *words*; it reduces itself to futile clamor, childishness, or lunacy. A performative utterance that is not an act does not exist. It has existence only as an act of authority. Now, acts of authority are first and always utterances made by those to whom the right to utter them belongs. This condition of validity, related to the person making the utterance and to the circumstances of the utterance, must always be considered met when one deals with the performative. The criterion is here and not in the choice of verbs. (236)

So certain has Benveniste become that words do things only by virtue of their users' status that this passage contradicts all he says elsewhere about the precise model of a declarative-jussive first-person present-tense verb: "The criterion is here and not in the choice verbs." He interrupts a fully developed argument for defining the performative linguistically to announce that the definition must be extra-linguistic, that it depends not on the *form* of an utterance but on "the *person* making the utterance and the *circumstances* of the utterance." Now the performative "does not exist" except as an act of authority undertaken by those with the requisite qualifications. When an unqualified person decrees general mobilization, Benveniste sees not an infelicitous performative but a void: "such an utterance is nothing at all"; "a performative utterance that is not an act does not exist."

It's clear what Benveniste is after when he gives social relationships rather than linguistic properties the power of life and death over the performative. If you're my boss and say *Come here,* I'm unlikely to ignore you because you forgot to say *I order.* As that example shows, however, when Benveniste brings social relationships in, he leaves no room at all for the "specific model" required by structuralist principles. The two sets of criteria don't supplement but exclude one another.

Benveniste's essay talks about society, and it talks about language. What it cannot do is put the two together. When the subject is language, the performative is purely linguistic; when the subject is society, it's purely social. While Austin's view of language and society as interactive is at the core of everything he says about both, Benveniste's categorical refusal of the interaction is at the core of all he says about either. Take the condemnation of the wrong person declaring general mobilization: "it cannot be an *act* . . . it's no more than *words.*" The emphasis is Benveniste's, and what is emphasized is an absolute opposition between the two things speech-act theory puts together.

What do you get if the wrong person tries to do things with words? Not a performative but "futile clamor, childishness, or lunacy." What do you get if the right person does things with the wrong words? Still not a performative, for we disqualify every utterance not fitting the "specific model, that of the verb in the present and in the first person" (237). The criteria are exact and rigid. Benveniste sees "no reason for abandoning the distinction between the performative and the constative" (238) because he imposes linguistic and social rules for the performative's existence that handle every problematic case by the effective strategy of declaring it non-existent.

The fascinating and instructive feature of this series of self-contradictory absolutes is that, despite insisting that the linguistic and non-linguistic are "two entirely different categories" (238), Benveniste is himself constrained to put the performative in *both.* He successively defines it in linguistic and non-linguistic terms and emphatically declares in each case that the criterion is here and nowhere else. Although even Homer sometimes nods, Benveniste is so intelligent and careful a scholar that there must be a compelling reason for his self-destructive argument. I take his apparent failure to see what he was doing as in fact the result of his seeing quite clearly that the performative is indeed linguistic and non-linguistic at once. He was scrupulous enough to report what he saw, but his structuralist axioms prevented him from recognizing and drawing the implications.

Both Benveniste's definitions therefore manifest the same refusal to put language and society together, and in both the quarrel is that Austin refuses to let them move apart. Besides excluding written signs like "Bridge Out" from the category of performatives, Benveniste eliminates the wrong sort of oral speech act as well: because there's no performative apart from the first-person declarative-jussive verb, if I lay my hand on the Bible and say "I will tell the truth, the whole truth, and nothing but the truth," I haven't sworn because I omitted the words "I swear." If you say you'll give me the money tomorrow or die trying, you haven't promised unless you introduced your commitment with "I promise."

Contrast this verbal pickiness to Austin's lackadaisicalness. In *How to Do Things with Words*, the conventions of Rule A.1 can perform with any words at all, can even dispense with words altogether: "many conventional acts, such as betting or conveyance of property, can be performed in non-verbal ways. The same sorts of rule must be observed in all such conventional procedures—we have only to omit the special reference to verbal utterance in our [Rule] A. This much is obvious" (Austin 1962; p. 19). What Austin finds "obvious" is unthinkable to Benveniste. From a structuralist perspective, every approach to language must accord primacy to precise linguistic features; Austin can do without them because illocutionary force depends on conventional rather than linguistic substance.

Benveniste understands society as no less fixed than language, and again the distance from Austin is striking. The person whose decree of general mobilization Benveniste dismissed could, given a state of revolutionary turmoil, produce a fully felicitous performative with exactly the same words and exactly the same absence of establishmentarian authority. All that's required is for a mass to mobilize itself in militant antagonism to those who once determined when it would march. Austin used a sports metaphor to make the point: "we have even the case of procedures which someone is initiating. Sometimes he may 'get away with it' like, in [rugby], the man who first picked up the ball and ran. Getting away with things is essential, despite the suspicious terminology" (Austin 1962; p. 30). Because collective conventions change, societies can both do things with whatever words they choose and make words do what they've never done before.

If the restricted performative is by itself enough to drive so gifted a scholar to so untenable a position as Benveniste's, imagine how much more of a challenge the generalized performative poses. Benveniste does manage to integrate the first-person declarative-jussive present-tense performative into the structuralist understanding of language as form not content, text not context. But there is obviously no way for a self-consistent structuralism to absorb Austin's final view that *all* utterances are illocutionary. Like the classic verbal statement, the classic verbal structure is stripped of its epistemological autonomy when we realize that it's *doing* something as well as *being* something. From Saussure to the present, this epistemological autonomy has been a given for all structuralist paradigms, including those applied to literature. Within speech-act paradigms, also including those applied to literature, it's a misconception.

Jerrold Katz, a scholar whose contributions to psycholinguistics are as impressive as Benveniste's to structuralism, is especially forthcoming about why restoring the performative/constative distinction and desocializing speech-act theory are a single move. Katz's *Propositional Structure and Illocutionary Force* bases itself on "Austin's promising idea, undercut by Austin's own hand" (Katz 1977; p. xiv) that the performative is special and unique.

For Katz, "Austin began with a set of neat, clean distinctions, for example, between constatives and performatives, but in the course of his investigations he undermined, blurred and erased almost all of them" (10). In order to keep the neat clarity and eliminate the blurry erasures—as he puts it, in order to show "how to save Austin from Austin" (177)—Katz reinstates the performative/constative distinction as thoroughly dependable. He then tries to codify the knowledge necessary for a speaker to do things with words by focusing exclusively on what Noam Chomsky calls "competence," the general set of rules internalized by all speakers of a language regardless of the circumstances where any particular speakers find themselves. This project constrains Katz to take the performative out of its social environment and envision it in the abstract. He erects an imaginary model "like Chomsky's ideal speaker-hearer or the physicist's perfect vacuum or frictionless plane" (14) and develops schematic representations for the model's efficacious operation.

The result is a version of speech-act theory to which the acts speech performs are explicitly irrelevant. "To construct this theory, the performance slant that Austin gave speech act theory had to be eliminated, and the basic idea of the theory had to be removed from the theory of acts and relocated in the theory of grammatical competence" (xii). Austin blurred and obliterated the "neat, clean distinctions" with which he began because of his awareness that society can dismantle logical categories no matter how stridently the rules of logic insist that they be kept whole. Katz's need to maintain distinctions leads him to set aside the collective propensity for joining together what thought puts asunder.

In transformational grammar, speakers' competence is unaffected by the errors they might make when they put their knowledge to work. "Performance" is transformational grammarians' term for the error-prone utterances of actual life, and failures in performance—slips of the tongue, stammers, second thoughts in mid-sentence—in no way invalidate the rules stored as linguistic competence. The patterns constituting grammatical ability are insulated from every existential contingency.

There's more than a lexical coincidence in the similarity of *performance*, which transformational grammar removes from consideration, and *performative*, which speech-act theory sets at the center of its project. Austin's subject was what we do with words in communities, not how we store and classify them in memory. Katz's attempt to eliminate "the performance slant that Austin gave speech-act theory" verges on rejecting everything the theory says. Austin believed that "an effect must be achieved on the audience if the illocutionary act is to be carried out" (116). Since the audience exists solely when there is a performance (an audience for competence is unthinkable), to eliminate the performance slant is to eliminate illocution as a category. And in speech-act theory, illocution is *the* category.

It would be hard to exaggerate the importance of the scholarly traditions represented by Katz and Benveniste. It's become common to speak of a "linguistic turn" in discipline after discipline because of the immense explanatory power of the models developed by structuralist and transformational research. Besides elucidating the nature of language, those two fields have inspired monumental contributions to scholarship throughout the human sciences.

Yet the fundamental breakthrough in both fields has been the decision to focus on language in itself, as a structure or a grammar, rather than on language in use, as human activity. Transformational grammar privileges competence over performance, structural linguistics addresses "language" instead of "speech," the forms all speakers of a language share rather than application of the forms to the situation created when two or more speakers get together. The linguistic turn is consequently a move away from concrete experience to abstract patterns.

Speech-act theory as Austin formulated it prohibits precisely this move. To understand how to do things with words, we cannot take the words away from the social environment in which the things get done. Even before making the point explicitly, *How to Do Things with Words* demonstrated the dual essence of speech acts—inextricably verbal and social at once—by the examples chosen to introduce the category. Austin's first three instances of what he wants to discuss clearly specify that performative utterances must be apprehended in combination with a conventional situation.

Examples:

> (E.*a*) "I do (sc. take this woman to be my lawful wedded wife)"—as uttered in the course of the marriage ceremony.
>
> (E.*b*) "I name this ship the *Queen Elizabeth*"—as uttered when smashing the bottle against the stem.
>
> (E.*c*) "I give and bequeath my watch to my brother"—as occurring in a will. (5)

In each case, the critical demand is that we envision speech and circumstances together. With the performative, we must know not only what is said but under which conditions, not only what is written but in what kind of document.

This of course doesn't mean that the structural and transformational characteristics of language become inoperative when words perform. Austin's validation of context doesn't repudiate but supplements language's abstract characteristics. The words that do things are the same words that Saussure, Chomsky, and their followers have explained, but the things done come from words' insertion into a specific social setting, no less determinant for their capacity to perform than the general properties of language for their capacity to mean.

Austinian integration of language and society, form and situation, is what Katz and Benveniste reject. Benveniste first defines the performative in sheerly verbal terms through the iron law of the first-person declarative-jussive present-tense verb, then establishes the iron law of social hierarchy without which performative speech is "nothing at all." Katz's elimination of the performance slant in Austin's work is exactly what he says, a necessary step toward producing a concept of speech acts to which the "theory of acts" has at most marginal pertinence. These encounters between Austin and linguistics clearly display the concerns that make Austin more than a linguist. Speech acts in society, and no trans-social schema can incorporate its illocutionary force.

Katz and Benveniste are by no means the only scholars for whom refusing Austin's unification of language and society entails refusing his unification of constative and performative at the same time. As Monique Schneider put it, if language is to be orderly "the performative must remain one linguistic category among others; the linguistic domain must be protected against the scandal of a general invasion by the performative of the territory of language as a whole" (1981; p. 32). The performative's unique status among linguistic utterances is incontrovertible when we consider it as we consider lexical structure and grammatical transformations, without interference from the vicissitudes of existence in historical time. Its uniqueness disappears only when we view all components of language in relation to their function in collective coexistence. A contextualized perspective makes it obvious that the constative is also performative, that words do things even when they also say things, that the patterns organizing logical theory cannot be transposed to the situations experienced in communal interaction. The constative/performative distinction, impeccably reliable when we consider language as a system, is indefensibly arbitrary when language interacts with people. There are good and valid reasons why students of language's systemic character don't accept Austin's renunciation of the great dividing line on which he began.

Formalist schools of literary criticism have understandably been thrilled by the determination of structural and transformational linguists to sever language from sociohistorical particularities. To concentrate on the text and the text alone also requires bracketing the vagaries of communities and studying a linguistic system in and of itself. As with linguistics, therefore, application of speech-act theory to literary analysis entails a fundamental shift in orientation.

The ways this shift has been accomplished will be the topic of this book's next section. Before addressing them, however, I have to confront an uncomfortable fact: Austin himself often denied that literary language figures among the words that do things. All critics— and there are many of us—who have found Austin's work invaluable have had to get around his own strictures against what we're doing. Austin was an "ordinary-language" philosopher, and in his opinion literature doesn't figure among language's ordinary uses. When words enter a text, he believes, they move beyond the reach of the social conventions with which they must interact in order to perform. Austin actually shares the formalist attitude toward literature his theory so decisively contests.

And that's why speech-act critics have not been deterred by Austin's admonitions: theory and theorist disagree over what literature is and does. The imperative to socialize that erases the dividing line between constative and performative also erases that between literary and performative. The only way to maintain an opposition between texts and speech acts is to separate texts from readers, and one of the most important lessons of *How to Do Things with Words* is the illegitimacy of every such abstraction of language from its users. To look at literature with speech-act principles in mind is to repeat the experience Benveniste had when he looked at the performative; again the discovery is that, even though we can say a great deal about formal properties in themselves, form alone cannot establish linguistic force. Society must come in when force is at issue, and with literature it certainly is.

For Austin, however, it's not. Illocution disappears, only locutions are left, when language is literary. The original delimitation of the performative in *How to Do Things with Words* specifies that it fails to act if we use it while joking or writing a poem, and Austin quickly extends his exclusion to other genres. His acts of exclusion are emphatic and unequivocal.

> A performative utterance will, for example, be *in a peculiar way* hollow or void if said by an actor on the stage, or if introduced in a poem, or spoken in soliloquy. This applies in a similar manner to any and every utterance—a sea-change in special circumstances. Language in such circumstances is in special ways—intelligibly— used not seriously, but in ways *parasitic* upon its normal use—ways which fall under the doctrine of the *etiolations* of language. All this we are *excluding* from consideration. Our performative utterances, felicitous or not, are to be understood as issued in ordinary circumstances. (22)

Literature is here "parasitic," "not serious," an enfeebled "etiolation" of language with the wiry sinews and red blood needed actually to perform an action. A copy rather than an original, an echo rather than speech, literary language is for the student of verbal performance no more than a photograph of the Himalayas for a mountaineer.

So why am I writing (and why are you reading) a book called *Speech Acts and Literary Theory*? Because Austin's concentration on words' power to do things in face-to-face oral exchange made him blind to the things done by written words in a literary text. Consider his repetition of literature's banishment from the house of illocution, especially the examples.

> We may speak of a "poetical use of language" as distinct from "the use of language in poetry." These references to "use of language" have

nothing to do with the illocutionary act. For example, if I say "Go and catch a falling star," it may be quite clear what both the meaning and the force of my utterance is, but still wholly unresolved which of these other kinds of things I may be doing. There are aetiolations, parasitic uses, etc., various "not serious" and "not full normal" uses. The normal conditions of reference may be suspended, or no attempt made at a standard perlocutionary act, no attempt to make you do anything, as Walt Whitman does not seriously incite the eagle of liberty to soar. (104)

Since the illocutionary act's defining feature is its conventionality, it's impossible to understand how so thoroughly conventionalized a language form as literature can have "nothing to do with the illocutionary act." Agreed that I don't do what Donne orders when I read his injunction to go and catch a falling star or get with child a mandrake root, why does that mean the *absence* of conventions rather than the *presence* of the conventions defining literary language? Those literary conventions would, say, invite me to *interpret* Donne's imperative rather than *execute* it through social processes identical in kind to those that invite an infantryman to execute a sergeant's imperative rather than interpret it. It's no more "natural" that I consider obeying some ordinary-language commands than that I don't consider obeying some commands found in literature. The entire thrust of Austin's thought is that words perform by virtue of the conventions social being applies to them. That fundamental insight is not compatible with his opinion of literature.

Even if Walt Whitman doesn't "seriously" incite the eagle of liberty to soar, the influence of Whitman's poetry in the history of American discourse on liberty is a very serious matter indeed, as is the capacity of that discourse to do things with substantive impact on the reality of American life. Although no bird out there answers to the name "eagle of liberty," even to suggest that there should be is to bring back the descriptive fallacy.

Two of Austin's capital insights are that the referent is not paramount and that perlocutionary behavior doesn't affect illocutionary identity. The contradictions between theory and theorist are blatant in the neglect of both insights when the quoted passage defines literature as a space where "the normal conditions of reference may be suspended, or no attempt made at a standard perlocutionary act." (By the way, C. Carroll Hollis [1983] begins his speech-act analysis of Whitman's poetry by quoting Austin's use of Whitman to show why there cannot be speech-act analyses of poetry; the irony is quite Austinian. To compound it, read Campbell [1975] and Levenston [1976] on the illocutionary status of Austin's other example of what illocution isn't, Donne's "Go and catch a falling star.")

Prominent in Austin's categorizations of literature is the word "normal," used as if literature's abnormality were universally and eternally self-evident. Yet all the rest of Austin's work argues that the norms applied to language are changeable conventions of social assessment instead of fixed inherent qualities. In the essay called "Performative-Constative," Austin specified that what passes for normal is of only marginal value to speech-act theory: "it is not in the least necessary that an utterance, if it is to be performative, should be expressed in one of these so-called normal forms" (1971; p. 16). Abnormal utterances can also be performative because the conventions of "so-called normal forms" are no more given in advance than any other kind.

Moreover, because the category of abnormality can come only from the *conventions* of normalcy, even to categorize literature as abnormal subjects it to Rule A.1. What Austin considered non-etiolated, full normal uses of the performative are far from the sole manifestation of conventional determination of linguistic force. Austin's expulsion of literature from the realm of speech acts ignores his own demonstrations that society establishes when speech fails to perform felicitously as well as when it succeeds.

Instead of a simple error on Austin's part, the line he draws between literary and performative language can be understood as a provisional step, exactly the same sort of rhetorical strategy deployed to set up the dividing line between constative and performative. The language Austin chooses to say that literature has nothing to do with the illocutionary act is no more definitive than the language he used to demarcate doing from saying, and that demarcation was set forth only to be repudiated. While Austin never did for the literary what he did for the constative—proclaim the speech-act character of what was originally excluded from speech-act theory—those of us who have ignored his strictures about literature are respecting the spirit of his writings as we ignore the letter.

That spirit highlights the multiple interactions between language and society, interactions that contest formalist concepts of the literary text as strongly as formalist concepts of the linguistic utterance. Regrettable though it is that Austin left the literature/illocution contrast intact, his example consistently shows why it should be smashed. Dismissal of the constative was a first step toward investigating the dynamic contact with collective being central to *all* language. Dismissal of the literary should have been a second step to the same end.

In an astute appreciation of the intersections between Austin's philosophy and Derridean deconstruction, Christopher Norris calls attention to the sections of *How to Do Things with Words* that violate other sections' prohibition of the literary. Austin uses many fictions in the interstices between his contentions that fictions don't belong. He wonders what particular form of infelicity made the language of the liturgy fail to take when the saint baptized the penguins, for example, and seems to get real pleasure from inventing scenarios about an effort to rename the *Queen Elizabeth* the *Mr. Stalin*. His other philosophical writings, full of elaborate tales like the one about a British officer in India who drove over a child's toy while rushing to quell an insurrection, sometimes explicitly state the necessity for narrative if speech-act theory is to get through; "the more we imagine the situation in detail, with a background of story," (Austin 1961; p. 184), he says, the more we will see how words and situation interact.

Literary examples help Austin make capital points throughout *How to Do Things with Words*, which invokes Don Quixote to show that the conventions of one age can become totally inactive in another. The central fact that sociohistorical conditions determine what ordinary language does is made through a character existing solely in literary language. Norris comments: "On the one hand, Austin is committed to maintaining the probity and real-life authority of speech-act utterance. On the other hand, he is everywhere obliged to resort to parables, analogies and illustrative fictions in order to explain his meaning" (1983b, p. 82). If we decline to accept Austin's definition of literature as non-serious, we have support in the many ideas of great seriousness he himself conveys through literary allusions and techniques.

As I am writing this, Salman Rushdie is in hiding and under heavy guard because of the death sentence pronounced on him by the Ayatollah Khomeini. Rushdie's offense was to publish the novel entitled *The Satanic Verses*, a work whose systematic stylistic and narrative violations of the rules for ordinary language furnish a particularly clear display of why literature might be excluded from language's "full normal" use. Tragically, however, Rushdie's text is also a stunning repudiation of Austin's opinion that literature, "hollow and void," is irrelevant to inquiry into verbal action. The language of *The Satanic Verses* is as immediately persuasive an example of words that do things as you could imagine. To set uncounted numbers of people on an assassin's task is a linguistic performance of titanic proportions.

I earlier used the ayatollah designating God's enemies as an exemplary instance of performative speech at its most pure. Like other governmental performatives, the Iranian hierarchy's fulminations against Rushdie demonstrate in a direct and unequivocal way that words do things on which life and death depend. Here there is no generalization of the performative, no blurring or erasure of the barrier separating it from the constative. The language saying that Rushdie had sinned against God and deserved to die did something monumental, something no one remotely concerned with speech acts can afford to exclude from consideration.

Yet this crystalline instance of the performative at its most immediately obvious was provoked by that which for Austin isn't connected with the performative at all, a literary text. The best possible example of the category has a perfectly extra-categorial origin, a conjunction of the clean and the unclean that problematizes every effort to keep them apart. For the same reason it would be silly to posit a conceptual barrier between two speech acts—Rushdie's novel and Khomeini's review—that are bound as cause and effect, it is foolish to deny any category of language the capacity to act. Like all utterances, the literary text becomes what collectivities make of it.

The horror of the Ayatollah's call for the death of the author because of his text is chilling. But it's also a reminder that literature is like every other verbal performance in deriving identity and force from socially specific assessments rather than from inherent trans-social qualities. Like a triple "I divorce you!" a novel does what conventions determine. One thing in Western democracies, *The Satanic Verses* is something quite different in Shiite Iran. Much as we may wish that freedom of literary expression were universal, that it is not makes it impossible to take the West's view of literature as coming from the essence of literature instead of the conventions of the West.

Authoritarian societies have of course always devoted special energy to assuring that literary words don't do things the regime dislikes; you can go to jail for your fictions as well as for violating what Austin would consider the normal performative obligations in contracts. Novelists' or playwrights' relative impunity from imprisonment because of their writings here and now says nothing about the nature of novels and plays elsewhere and at other times. The text too enacts a collectivity.

For literature is an illocutionary act even if its illocutionary force is vastly different from that of ordinary language. What Austin called the "sea-change in special circumstances" that occurs when words become literary is as much a social production as the special circumstances prevailing before the change occurs. Literature is defined by the conventions organizing the community that recognizes it as literature. The text too does things through and with those to whom it speaks.

The immense majority of texts of course do nothing remotely so dramatic as *The Satanic Verses*. But then most "ordinary" utterances do nothing remotely so dramatic as "I do." Once overt performatives have displayed the interactions between language and society, it becomes obvious that other verbal forms are dynamic social forces as well. The constative/performative and literary/illocution distinctions are equally irreconcilable with recognition that what language says is as much a speech act as what it does. Like saying and doing, writing performs.

Part II

Applications

4

Austin and Searle Together and Apart

"How in the world do I handle John Searle?" has been running through my mind as a nagging as well as vaguely poetic question ever since I first had the idea of writing this book. There was no hesitation over *whether* to include him. His work, constantly cited by literary critics as well as philosophers, has towering stature among scholars interested in speech acts. My problem was *how* to include him, for his great contributions to spreading Austin's ideas through the academic community have from the beginning been inseparable from explicit and implicit departures from Austin that impede adaptation of speech-act theory to literary purposes.

So I wrote the first part of this book without mentioning Searle even though there were many points where his work deserved (positive or negative) introduction. My knowledge of his most significant arguments, those that repeat and refine Austin's work, was invaluable as I organized my own exposition of *How to Do Things with Words* in the first part of this book. I credit him here instead of there because earlier introduction of his developments of Austin would have meant introducing criticisms as well, and those criticisms are irrelevant to the foundation Austin laid.

The points on which Austin and Searle disagree, and the scholars who share my opinion that their disagreements should almost always be resolved in Austin's favor, will acquire sharper focus as this book proceeds. At present, I want to consider what students of literature have taken from Searle's work and how he has himself addressed literary topics. Although Searle has suggested that literary critics always get it wrong, his own work gets it right often enough to deserve a chapter in this study of speech acts in literary criticism.

Searle's most serviceable refinement of Austin is his systematization of speech-act types, which substitutes a five-part schema for the complex (not to say chaotic) classification Austin tentatively put forward in the last of the lectures collected in *How to Do Things with*

Words. Almost all critics who have looked at the different kinds of illocution represented in literature have taken Searle's schema over Austin's list, for the advantages are multiple. Searle's taxonomy (1979; pp. 12–20) posits five varieties of illocution. The constative becomes the "assertive," and Austin's multiple categories of the performative are reduced to four: directives (*I order, I beg*), commissives (*I promise, we pledge*), expressives (*I apologize, Thanks a lot*) and declarations (the whole set of institutionally based exercises of verbal authority already extensively discussed here).

Searle systematically lays out his version of illocutionary analysis in *Speech Acts: An Essay in the Philosophy of Language*, which appeared in 1969. For students of literature, the thorniest aspect of *Speech Acts* is its proclivity for the abstract notation of logical analysis—Searle represents the general form of illocution not by discussing society and conventions but by writing "F(p)," for example—and for positing the simplified context on which this notation depends. Although Searle has forcefully rejected the extra-contextual formalization favored by transformational grammarians like Jerrold Katz, he has also implicitly agreed with Katz that speech-act theory should follow the lead of the natural sciences and assume impossibilities like a frictionless plane to explain the actualities of the world. This is from Searle's introduction to his description of the promise, which his *Speech Acts* takes to represent all illocutions.

> I am going to deal only with a simple and idealized case. This method, one of constructing idealized models, is analogous to the sort of theory construction that goes on in most sciences, e.g., the construction of economic models, or accounts of the solar system which treat planets as points. Without abstraction and idealization there is no systematization. (56)

Despite Austin's refusal of the simple situations envisaged in logical theory, Searle takes them as the starting point for his explanation of how to do things with words.

Since literature produces situations that logical theory customarily ignores, literary critics have with reason been leery of programmatic devotion to abstraction, idealization, and systematization. Fortunately, though, Searle also provides concrete principles of broad value for literary criticism. He shares Austin's conviction that to study language as form without attending to the form's function within human lives is a self-defeating futility. Even though he takes construction of economic models as an example to be emulated, for example, Searle also sharply criticizes economists who classify a community's currency without noticing that money helps the community's members get through the day (17). Despite his commitment to the sometimes hermetic discourse of analytic philosophy, despite his reservations about literary critics' ability to handle speech-act paradigms, Searle's vision of language in the world holds important lessons for textual analysis.

One of the pivotal lessons in *Speech Acts* is the distinction between brute facts and institutional facts, a needed expansion of the idea Austin expressed as the difference between kicking a ball and kicking a goal. Brute facts, wholly independent of conventions, are best exemplified by physical realities: what balls do when a foot hits them with a certain momentum, what happens to water at a certain temperature. Institutional facts are on the contrary conventionally determined. "They are indeed facts; but their existence, unlike the existence of brute facts, presupposes the existence of human institutions" (Searle 1969; p. 51). When a ball scores a goal, the brute fact of the momentum imparted to it by a foot is of a different order from the institutional fact that it changes the relative standing of the two sides in the game.

Searle's other examples of institutional facts include a couple's marriage, a defendant's conviction, the result of a baseball game, passage of a Congressional act. In each, something real takes its reality solely from the socio-institutional dynamics prevailing at a given time and place. Institutional facts are in no way less substantial or important than brute facts. It's a brute fact that George Bush has two big toes, an institutional fact that he was elected President of the United States of America. For the world at large, probably even for George Bush, the institutional fact is easily the more consequential. That illocutionary force is an institutional fact in no way diminishes it.

The category of institutional facts is closely bound up with what Searle calls "constitutive rules," those that can't be violated under penalty of abolishing the activity to which they apply. Constitutive rules are opposed to "regulative rules," which may govern but do not *constitute* a form of behavior. When two teams from the National Football League meet on a Sunday afternoon, the home team has first choice of what color jersey to wear. That rule is regulative; nothing about the game of football would be different if the visiting team got to choose jerseys. The rules governing what counts as a valid play, however, are constitutive. Ignore or alter them and the game is no longer what it was.

Constitutive rules are institutional rather than brute facts, and their importance shows that brute facts alone are woefully insufficient. Without constitutive rules, we would not only lose the games we play, we would undermine the lives we lead. Rules give us social existence as well as touchdowns, the ability to coexist as well as the chance to checkmate. The things they constitute are necessary to our own survival as well as to that of our games.

Searle uses concepts like constitutive rules to repudiate inherited ideas about language's primary responsibility to describe the brute facts of the extra-linguistic world. His dismissal of the descriptive fallacy is decisive: "These are the only two plausible ways of applying the theory of descriptions to all kinds of illocutionary acts. Neither works. The theory should, therefore, be abandoned" (162). When institutional facts are at issue, as they always are with human beings, we get nowhere by proceeding as if brute facts were all.

Like Austin, Searle shows that many standard philosophical principles become inapplicable when we come to see the distinction between language in the world and language in the abstract. Since Wittgenstein, a tautological assertion like "Either it's raining or it's not" has been generally considered void. Because tautologies are always true, no tautology says anything worth mentioning; because none says anything, all tautologies are equivalent and interchangeable. Searle contends that "nothing could be further from the truth" (124) than to assume that tautological identity exempts us from considering the existential variety inseparable from actual use of language, including tautological language.

His evidence is the clear distinction—the obvious lack of equivalence and interchangeability—between two other tautological sentences, "Either he's a Communist or he isn't" and "Either he's a Fascist or he isn't." While it's true that no assertion is made in one or the other (both are true about every "he"), the first tautology suggests the possibility of left-wing extremism, the second that of right-wing extremism. Each therefore performs the speech act of suggestion, and few politicians would be indifferent to the suggestion made.

This contrast between tautologies is convincing because the Fascist and Communist examples introduce the speech-act matrix of sociohistorical specificity in a way Wittgenstein's raining example fails to do; the facts of Fascism and Communism are clearly institutional rather than brute, and their rhetorical impact no less clearly depends on the conventions Austin codified in Rule A.1. Interestingly, though, Searle does nothing with this feature of his argument, which is typical of his general strategy to pay little attention to the social specificity of illocution. An accepted conventional procedure with conventional effect was for Austin conceptually as well as alpha-numerically first. In Searle, it's less important.

As we saw, *How to Do Things with Words* deduces all the other rules for performative force from Rule A.1. Searle's *Speech Acts* takes over the idea of a principal condition that "determines the others" (69), but now what is called the "essential rule" in every illocution is what the particular utterance "counts as" (63, 66–67). "I'll be there at seven" counts as a promise if it commits me to be there at the time I said, but it might also count as a question if I say it in such a way that it leads you to tell me what time you're coming, or as a request if what I'm after is to get you to come at the same time. Although Searle's essential rule is patently an institutional fact and as such depends on conventions, he chooses not to foreground conventional determination with anything like Austin's assertiveness.

I see this difference as related to Searle's decision to direct attention to *individual performance* rather than *collective production* of speech acts. It's apparent throughout most of Searle's writings that what an utterance counts as is not some absolute given but rather the effect of a community establishing and enforcing its particular form of coexistence. The concluding words of *Speech Acts* make the point strongly: "speaking a language—as has been the main theme of this book—consists of performing speech acts according to rules, and there is no separating those speech acts from the commitments which form essential parts of them" (198). The rules and commitments accepted whenever we speak come from the conventions that apply because we always speak in definite sociohistorical circumstances.

Nevertheless, Searle's emphasis on what an utterance counts as over the conventions through which it comes to count has the effect of devaluing the Austinian dialectic between illocutionary force and social identity. This change in emphasis leads to curious instances of completely asocial performatives. For example, while discussing declarations in "A Taxonomy of Illocutionary Acts," Searle admits a divine exception to the requirement that only people with definite positions in social institutions can declare war, declare a couple married, or produce any of the other reality-transforming utterances institutions make possible: "there are supernatural declarations. When, e.g., God says 'Let there be light' that is a declaration" (1979; p. 18). To the contrary, divine beings are totally incapable of performative speech, which is accomplished solely by the protocols organizing *human* communities. God stands outside those communities, conventions are radically inapplicable to Him or Her, the norms of social interaction fail to reach heaven. "Let there be light" and a human sentence that also does what it says have nothing else in common.

Confusion of the illocutionary and the supernatural is consistent with Searle's general move away from the set toward society in *How to Do Things with Words*. God's declarative power is part of an argument leading to this distancing of Searle's version of speech-act theory from Austin's: "Austin sometimes talks as if all performatives (and in the general theory, all illocutionary acts) required an extra-linguistic institution, but this is plainly not the case" (18). If God can do without institutional support, the passage implies, so can analysis of the specifically human force called illocution.

Austin's suggestions are valid or not depending on our understanding of "institution." If the word designates a specific organization with full bureaucratic credentials, then Searle is correct to distinguish between declarations like those producing a law or a state of siege from more homespun performatives like those making a bet or an apology; the institutional investiture required for a declaration to be felicitous isn't necessary for an apology to be made.

But if we understand institutions in the broader sense—in just the sense brought forward in Searle's category of *institutional* facts—then it plainly is the case that the way "Austin sometimes talks" represents the way Austin always thinks. In the looser sense, extra-linguistic institutions permeate not only bureaucratic organization but all the protocols—all the institutional facts—establishing and preserving a social formation. Institutions can well be understood as neither more nor less than the sum of the conventions that invariably make speech act.

Searle's peremptory announcement that Austin is "plainly" wrong about extra-linguistic institutions may indicate discomfort with "extra-linguistic" as well as "institution." Austin and Searle certainly share an understanding of speech acts as deriving from social organization rather than from qualities inherent to language. Yet the extra-linguistic almost always attains greater prominence in Austin. The difference between Rule A.1 in *How to Do Things with Words* and the essential rule in *Speech Acts* is that between the prior social reality necessary for speech to act and the present definition of the act performed. In one case, we must consider a conventional interaction as the first step toward validly apprehending a linguistic utterance; in the other, we begin with the utterance. The distinction is subtle but consequential. Despite Austin and Searle's fundamental agreement, they assign different value to the collective construction of illocutionary felicity.

Searle's diminished concern with society has strong impact on his definition of the problematics appropriate to a speech-act consideration of literature. The essay called "The Logical Status of Fictional Discourse" follows the lead of a brief discussion in *Speech Acts* by taking the primary question posed by the intersection of illocution and literature to be not how literature is related to society but how fiction is different from lies. Comparing a passage from the *New York Times* to a passage from Iris Murdoch's novel *The Red and the Green*, Searle points out that both passages consist principally of assertions. Yet neither the essential rule for assertions nor any derivative rules apply to the novel, whereas all apply to the newspaper. Searle's goal is to explain the "logical status" of this apparent breakdown of the constitutive rules for asserting felicitously.

To reach that goal, Searle appropriates the banal idea that authors are "pretending" to say things. Fiction consists of pretending without any wish to be taken seriously, and in Searle's view production of what looks like lies but isn't results from fiction's articulation with a set of conventions that "suspend the normal requirements" (66) imposed by the rules applying to assertions elsewhere. Searle calls the two sets of conventions, one committing the speaker to be truthful, the other removing that commitment, "vertical" and "horizontal." His argument is that normal, vertical conventions continue to function as the source of meaning even though the fictional, horizontal sort insulates the author from responsibility for what's being said. "What distinguishes fiction from lies is the existence of a separate set of conventions which enables the author to go through the motions of making statements which he knows to be not true even though he has no intention to deceive" (67).

This set of pretending conventions allows us to distinguish logically between statements like "Sherlock Holmes lived in London" and "Sherlock Holmes had a blonde wife." In one sense, neither assertion is true, for there never was a Sherlock Holmes. But in the sense made possible by recognizing specifically fictional conventions, it's true that Sherlock Holmes lived in London and false that he had a wife. We can refer to fictional worlds for the same reason we can refer to actual worlds, because illocutionary understanding gives us the capacity to do so. It's of no special interest that the enabling conventions are not identical; what matters is that they are indeed enabling.

Yet I have real problems understanding how this will help me as a reader of fiction. Assuming that there do exist pretense conventions analogous to conventions for promising and declaring, how do we internalize and apply them? While reading a particular work, do we know when the pretending conventions are in effect and when their suspending power is itself suspended? Since countless fictional works refer to real people, places, and events while also pretending, how can we tell when words obey normal referring conventions and when they abrogate them? While Searle says that his model applies to "fictional discourse," which always pretends, rather than to works of fiction, which sometimes don't, he offers no advice on how to tell when a work of fiction abandons fictional discourse for something else.

Searle suggests one aspect of the problem when he considers the famous opening remark in *Anna Karenina* that happy families are all alike, each unhappy family miserable in its own way: "That, I take it, is not a fictional but a serious utterance" (74). Searle doesn't explain *how* he came to "take it" that this was a real assertion; however, since he finds Tolstoy "tiresomely didactic" (74), the reason is presumably that the first sentence of *Anna Karenina* purports to teach a lesson about the world without mentioning Anna or other characters. My problem as a reader is this: given that subsequent mention of characters seems integrally related to the novel's first sentence, fictional and serious discourse are in tight *thematic* connection despite what Searle considers their *illocutionary* discontinuity. If the fictional takes off from the serious, if the serious categorizes the fictional, how do I know when to "take it" that speech-act conventions have been changed, and why should I care?

Charles Dickens's *A Tale of Two Cities* presents a different problem. This novel sets its characters in Paris at the time of the French Revolution, and its assertions about (imaginary) characters are almost always at the same time assertions about the (real) French Revolution. The distinction between fictional and serious discourse is obviously untenable if a given stretch of discourse is both, and *A Tale of Two Cities* is one of countless novels in which a fictional/serious hybrid is the norm. By no means is the difficulty limited to real places like Paris or real events like the September massacres of 1792. It can permeate every word in the novel with the (possible) exception of those that designate imaginary characters by name or pronoun.

The sentence that begins Dickens's last chapter is an instance: "Along the Paris streets the death carts rumble, hollow and harsh." Death carts to the guillotine are among the novel's more powerful evocations of revolutionary terror. They (and the noise they make) are as concrete a reference to reality as the "Paris streets" they rumble along. Yet *these* death carts have Sydney Carton and other imaginary characters in them, which makes them just-pretend things that annul the same serious discourse they're in the process of producing. Within Searle's schema, normal illocutionary conventions must often apply and not apply at the same time.

Even if application and suspension are sequential not simultaneous, it's hard to imagine an author with enough illocutionary stamina to make it through a novel when writing one demands constant vigilance to keep the status of speech acts clear. Just to get out "Reader, I married him" Brontë had to assume four successive illocutionary attitudes: Reader (*normal conventions apply*) I (*normal conventions suspended*) married (*normal conventions apply*) him (*normal conventions suspended*). The illocutionary effect of authorial pretending is thoroughly implausible.

For Austinian criticism, it's also thoroughly unnecessary. Speech-act theory came into being when Austin recognized that accurate or inaccurate description of referents was *not pertinent* to how words do things. By taking the referential validity of literary assertions as his paramount concern, Searle brings the descriptive fallacy back into speech-act theory. The question for an Austinian critic is not when the language of *A Tale of Two Cities* refers but how it performs. In Dickens the French Revolution is a constative presence rather than a referential fact, characters a constative identity instead of a referential failure. One of Austin's great lessons for literary scholars is that the constative too repudiates the descriptive fallacy, and confusing the constative and the referential means this lesson hasn't been learned.

This sentence suggests another reason Searle's schema can't help in literacy criticism: "To the extent that the author is consistent with the conventions he has invoked or (in the case of revolutionary forms of literature) the conventions he has established, he will remain within the conventions" (Searle 1979; p. 73). How can readers apply Searle's concept of authorial suspension of illocutionary conventions when all they know is that it apples when it applies? "To the extent that the author is consistent with the conventions [. . .] he will remain within the conventions." In *Speech Acts*, Searle made the excellent point that "from tautologies only tautologies follow" (106). That principle certainly holds for conventions and suspensions that either are or aren't in force when a reader encounters a work of fiction.

But Searle is avowedly indifferent to what happens when a reader encounters a work of fiction. His sole concern is what happens when an author produces one. In a strategy he would broaden in his book *Intentionality*, Searle makes authorial purpose the *sole* determining factor in identifying fiction; only pretending counts, and the author alone can make himself or herself pretend. Searle's insistence on this point is categorical, as is his dismissal of literary scholars who see the reader's interaction with a text as meaningful.

> The identifying criterion for whether or not a text is a work of fiction must of necessity lie in the illocutionary intentions of the author. There is no textual property, syntactical or semantic, that will identify a text as a work of fiction. What makes it a work of fiction is, so to speak, the illocutionary stance that the author takes toward it, and

> that stance is a matter of the complex illocutionary intentions that
> the author has when he writes or otherwise composes it. (65–66)

In Austinian speech-act theory, illocutionary force is the work of a community. Searle restricts it to an individual, the single person whose illocutionary *intentions* are all by themselves able to suspend the illocutionary *conventions* that govern linguistic performance for the rest of the world. His essay on literature is therefore consonant with Searle's general deemphasis of the collective character of illocution; his approach to fiction purposely and purposefully ignores fiction's circulation within a community.

For the purposes of this book, what matters is that, even though Searle's venture into literary analysis has nothing to say to literary critics, the reason for the failure lies not in speech-act theory but in its idiosyncratic application. When Searle allows a single person's will to invalidate a community's speech-act rules, he makes illocution radically different from what it is in Austin. "The [illocutionary] act is constituted not by intention" (Austin 1962; p. 128). Like all the other things we do with words, fiction exists by communal ratification.

In a nuanced version of Searle's position, Brown and Steinmann make the point that "a discourse *is* fictional because its speaker or writer intends it to be so. But it is *taken as* fictional only because its hearer or reader *decides* to take it so" (1978; p. 149). Whatever we think of the equation between individual intention and what a discourse *is*, it's essential to see that *taking* the discourse in a certain way is the only active component during the reading experience. Even if readers assume the author's intention is all-determining, their assumption is still a feature of how they take literature rather than of how literature *is*.

Searle's contention that authorial intention can switch fiction on and off like a lamp runs counter to everything he says elsewhere about how language "counts as" any form of illocution. As Stanley Fish points out in his discussion of Searle's "Logical Status of Fictional Discourse," "the distinction between serious and fictional discourse [. . .] cannot be maintained if the implications of speech-act theory are clearly and steadily seen" (Fish 1980; p. 197).

Despite the problems with its view of fiction, Searle's essay discusses *literature* in a way that *does* clearly and steadily see the implications of speech-act theory. While defining fiction as the exclusive production of the author, Searle also defines literature as the consequence of the collective assessment central to illocution. He puts the distinction this way: "Roughly speaking, whether or not a work is literature is for the readers to decide, whether or not it is fiction is for the author to decide" (59). It's part of Searle's general desocializing strategy that he takes this difference as urging attention to fiction, which he sees as an individually established entity, rather than literature, the social production of readers' decision. An Austinian critic would take the opposite course and argue that literature, for Searle "the name of a set of attitudes we take toward a stretch of discourse, not a name of an internal property of the stretch of discourse" (59), is an obvious candidate for speech-act analysis. It is after all speech-act theory that taught us not to look for the force of language in "an internal property" but rather in a "set of attitudes," in that which defines whether "The window's open" states, warns, requests, or actualizes one of the many other illocutionary potentialities its locutionary properties can never tell us anything about. Insofar as it derives from Austin's Rule A.1, speech-act theory is attuned to the influence of communal assessments like those defining literature. Searle's lack of interest in Rule A.1 leads him to take the entity established by communal assessment to be a topic he can comfortably ignore.

Searle has little respect for literary criticism or those who practice it. "The Logical Status of Fictional Discourse" sees such key critical concepts as "mimesis" to be nothing but "catchphrases" that critics repeat to make it "easy to stop thinking" (60). Searle believes that "theorists of literature are prone to make vague remarks" (73), and he takes satisfaction that his own work has finally put the world in a "position to make sense of those remarks" (73).

In the face of such barbs, the temptation for us critics is to point out that even philosophers can sometimes stop thinking long enough to write an essay proving that authors remain within the conventions to the extent that they are consistent with the conventions. Searle's claim to have solved the problem of fictionality has little basis beyond his decision to call fiction "pretending," a fine instance of the magical rather than the Austinian method of doing things with words.

To riposte in that way, however, would ignore Searle's exemplary point about the importance for *literary* understanding of the set of attitudes prevailing in a community. Like much of his work, "The Logical Status of Fictional Discourse" has important things to say to critics. Literary scholars have fruitfully applied Searle as well as Austin in developing the speech-act criticism discussed in the following chapters, and ultimately the lessons we have learned from him count more than the lessons it's better to skip.

5

Textual Illocution

To adopt a speech-act perspective on literary texts (rather than on fictional discourse) is to see that literature, like any other linguistic performance, is a collective interaction as well as a verbal object. Like any other linguistic performance, therefore, literature is illuminated rather than impoverished when its interpreters consider it in relation to its users. Although there's no shortage of critical schools that argue with seductive vigor for the text's absolute and sacrosanct locutionary autonomy, a speech-act vision requires that we focus rather on the text's illocutionary force. Since the fundamental starting point for every Austinian inquiry is the collectively sustained conventions that enable words to do things, to consider literature as illocution is also to consider the societies from which it comes and in which it circulates.

This socialized criticism can address two principal topics, the status of literature in general and the status of the separate utterances making up a given text. In the seventies, Richard Ohmann and Mary Louise Pratt both chose the first topic and published important efforts to develop a global definition of literature through speech-act categories. Ohmann most systematically discussed textual illocution in an essay that announces its global concern in its title, "Speech Acts and the Definition of Literature."

Ohmann provocatively argues that we can and should combine two seeming irreconcilables: 1) Austin's insistence that literature is not a speech act; 2) literary criticism based on Austin's vision of language in society. To bring the two together, Ohmann defines literature as a "quasi-speech-act." "Quasi" recognizes the distinction between words in a text and words in the world, "speech act" proclaims that words in a text nevertheless interact with the social reality of conventional procedures and conventional effects.

In Ohmann's view, the multiple efforts throughout the history of Western aesthetics to distinguish literature from other verbal forms have all concentrated either on locutionary or perlocutionary features; none has addressed literature's illocutionary being. Some theorists have posited the defining trait as the text's capacity to elicit a heightened emotional reaction from its readers; what makes a work literary is the perlocutionary fact that those who read it respond with feeling despite the work's disconnection from the existential circumstances that usually stimulate human emotion. Other theorists have believed that what counts is the rich variety of literature's structures, the complex set of elements constituting it as a locution with a far denser verbal texture than non-literary utterances.

Ohmann rejects both approaches to make the same argument about literature that Austin made about language: those who have addressed it have attended to locution (what it is) or perlocution (how it feels) rather than to illocution, what it does in connection with the conventional procedures through which it operates. Ohmann schematically divides the works of previous theorists into six schools and contends that only a speech-act perspective can avoid their fundamental error and give textual illocution its due.

> The six definitions I considered earlier fall into two classes: those that focus on the text itself, along with its reference, its verity, and its meaning (locutionary definitions); and those that focus on its effects (perlocutionary definitions). Given the ubiquity of conventions in and around literary discourse, I think it promising to look for an illocutionary definition. (10)

In other terms, literary creation and appreciation belong among the conventions of Rule A.1. The point of departure for Ohmann's "Speech Acts and the Definition of Literature" is that Austin's insights into language are applicable to literature as well.

Immediately after this capital point, however, Ohmann extends his agreement with Austin to assert that the work of literature is not an illocutionary act. He lists Austin's conditions for felicitous illocution and says that literature violates them all. Two lines from a Richard Eberhart poem simultaneously typify literary discourse and violate each Austinian characterization of performative discourse. The problems with Eberhart would for Ohmann disqualify any literary utterance from performing in an Austinian sense, and as a result literature's defining feature is its sheer otherness beside every variety of non-literary language.

> I am ready to set down the first approximation of a definition: *a literary work is a discourse abstracted, or detached, from the circumstances and conditions which make illocutionary acts possible; hence*

it is a discourse without illocutionary force. (Austin suggests as much
by saying that a poem is a "parasitic" use of language, in which the
illocutionary forces undergo "etiolation.") (13)

Because illocutionary force is the foundation and armature of
speech-act theory, because it is in fact consubstantial with the speech
act itself, there is a daunting conceptual hurdle to be overcome here:
an essay entitled "Speech Acts and the Definition of Literature," an
essay that says it intends to "look for an illocutionary definition" of
the literary work, nevertheless presents literature as "a discourse
without illocutionary force." Ohmann therefore immediately qualifies
what sounds like an absolute opposition and gives literature at least
an imitative illocutionary status. "Let me supplement the definition:
*A literary work is a discourse whose sentences lack the illocutionary
forces that would normally attach to them. Its illocutionary force is
mimetic.* By 'mimetic,' I mean purportedly imitative" (14).

"Purported imitation" is vital to Ohmann's vision of literature as a
"quasi-speech-act." The literary work *purports* to imitate illocutions
that are in fact non-existent, that are therefore not speech acts in the
ordinary sense. Yet readers respond to those quasi-speech-acts as
humans always respond to words that do things, by orienting themselves to the conventions that determine the things done. The consequence is that the reader constructs a world by imagining which of
that world's conventions would permit speech to act in the purportedly determinant way. "A literary work calls on all a reader's competence as decipherer of speech acts" (15), but instead of deriving illocutionary force from a social whole, the reader constructs a social whole
from what purports to be illocutionary force.

The literary work provides "an indefinitely detailed imaginary setting for its quasi-speech-acts" (14), confronts readers "with impaired
and incomplete speech acts" that they must complete "by supplying
the appropriate circumstances" (17). What the text leaves "indefinitely
detailed" acquires definition through the reader's instinctive knowledge of how Rule A.1 operates outside the textual realm. Because
they are "impaired and incomplete," literary locutions are only *quasi*-
speech-acts. But we must not forget that works of literature are quasi-
speech-acts; they require readers to give the substance of fully operative conventions to language that lacks it.

On the one hand, by positing a gap between literature and ordinary
language, Ohmann accepts Austin's position that literature doesn't
belong among the topics speech-act theory can fruitfully consider.
The theory's ground is the conviction that we can understand language only if we see it as the dynamically illocutionary agent of human

interaction, and one part of Ohmann's argument represents literature as neither dynamic nor illocutionary: "the quasi-speech-acts of literature are not carrying on the world's business—describing, urging, contracting, etc." (17). Literature therefore doesn't do a single one of the things Austin showed words to be capable of doing.

On the other hand, however, everything Austin adduced to explain how to do things with words comes into play in the second part of Ohmann's definition. "In inviting the reader to constitute speech acts to go with its sentences, the literary work is asking him to participate in the imaginative construction of a world" (17). Although literature here contains only "sentences" whereas the rest of language consists of "speech acts," readers' knowledge that sentences and speech acts—locution and illocution—are elsewhere identical makes them seek just that identity in the text as well. If their quest is to succeed, they must provide the world the text lacks. "Mimesis" thus becomes production, production oriented by every language user's instinctive recognition that speech is interwoven with human coexistence.

"Speech Acts and the Definition of Literature" first sets the text so apart from society that literature is a discourse without illocutionary force, which for speech-act theory is a discourse outside human communities. But Ohmann's "supplement" to his denial of the text as illocution, socialized through and through, takes complete advantage of the fact that *reading* always occurs in human communities even if the *text* manages to find a home somewhere else. Each aspect of readers' "imaginative construction of a world" derives directly from their knowledge of how language functions in a collectivity. Like Austin, Ohmann distinguishes between literary texts and words that actually do things. But when, unlike Austin, Ohmann applies a speech-act perspective to literary works, he immediately asserts that doing the world's business and telling the world's stories are intimately connected rather than rigidly opposed. Faced with pure textual "sentences," Ohmann's reader constitutes speech acts to fill the void. In the process, illocution occupies the whole of the space from which it was originally banned. Ohmann's ultimate affirmation of textual illocution is a clear instance of awareness that words do things leading straight to awareness of literature's social identity.

In the essay called "Literature as Act," Ohmann develops the socialized supplement to his original definition and gives more prominence to the productive effect of readers' experience within collectivities during their contact with a text. Because language's illocutionary status drives us to infuse a social function into any literary utterances that seem not to present one, *communal* interaction is integral to the *individual* reading experience. Ohmann's new formulation, that "mimesis draws into play the reader's social self" (1973; p. 99), leads to refusal of all critical orientations that foreground asocial aspects of selfhood, such as the reader's psyche or transcendent aesthetic sensibility.

In Ohmann's "Literature as Act," the mechanism activated during the reading process remains the imaginative construction of a world out of the sensation that only such a world can enable speech to do what the text represents it as doing. But the later essay goes much farther in considering the consequences for readers (and for teachers) of the mimetic knowledge in play. Each reader's social self varies across several registers, notably those created by gender, class, and race. Therefore "the participation of readers in mimesis will properly differ" (104), and the key word is "properly." The socialized fields of reader-response criticism develop in tandem with the speech-act vision of what brings readers to respond at all. Ohmann ultimately focuses much more insistently on the ways literature interacts with the world than on the ways it shuts itself off.

Nevertheless, the original definition of literature as inactive remains as disquieting in Ohmann as it was in Austin. The intersection of speech-act theory and literary analysis provides little place for even ephemeral assertions that literature is what illocution is not. In *Toward a Speech-Act Theory of Literary Discourse* (1977), Mary Louise Pratt argues with committed intensity that all oppositions between literature and ordinary language result from misapprehending both. While Pratt's primary theoretical foundation comes not from Austin but from other philosophers of language, especially H. P. Grice, her ideas have been an important channel for propagating speech-act theory among literary scholars. She never equivocates in her insistence on using all we know of language in society to help us understand language in literature.

Pratt's favorite target is what she calls the Poetic Language Fallacy. Invented by Russian Formalists, Prague School linguists, and other structuralist groups, the doctrine of poetic language holds certain qualities to be unique to literary enunciation. Although the requisite traits have been variously defined, central to all definitions is the idea that the traits chosen cohere to form "literariness," something constitutive of literature and absent from all other linguistic forms. For partisans of poetic language, insight into ordinary language is patently irrelevant because literature is by definition *sui generis*.

Pratt's repudiation of literariness is sweeping. As she states in her preface and shows throughout her book, there is no valid reason to assume that language stops being itself when it enters a literary work. On the contrary, "it is both possible and necessary [. . .] to talk about literature in the same terms we use to talk about all the other things people do with language" (vii). Poetic-language doctrines always imply that the text transcends society to become non- or omni-contextual; Pratt's speech-act doctrine advances rather "a view of literature as a linguistic activity which cannot be understood apart from the context in which it occurs and the people who participate in it" (viii). *How to Do Things with Words* made the same argument about non-literary discourse and amply laid out the reasons linguistic understanding depends on the people who communicate with one another and the context in which their exchange occurs. While Austin is not her reference of choice, Pratt's insistence on the fact that the meaningful context of utterances is always the world of human interaction is an exemplarily Austinian position.

One way to protect literariness is to concentrate on the features through which literature directs attention to itself and away from everything surrounding its composition and consumption. Definition of those features has made a momentous contribution to influential criticism throughout the twentieth century, and Pratt never denies the value of critical sensitivity to a text's self-absorption. Her position that the concept of poetic language is fallacious in no way refuses the character and strength of the linguistic resources on which poetry traditionally relies. She simply denies that these resources are unique to literature. The objectionable aspect of cataloguing a text's allusions to its own textuality is the assumption—explicit as often as implicit—that what is being catalogued can be discerned only in a limited set of verbal utterances. The fallacious component of the Poetic Language Fallacy is not the devices it perceives in poetry but its inability to recognize that these same devices are also critical to other things done with words: celebrate literariness all you want, but never make the mistake of believing it's found only in literature. For Pratt, poetic-language critics err less in their representation of poetry than in their "drastic misrepresentation of nonliterary discourse" (xii).

Pratt argues that even Ohmann's speech-act definition of literature lapses into this misrepresentation. To call literature a quasi-speech act is to ignore that ordinary language often displays each feature that could be adduced to justify the *quasi*. Every one of the traits posited as unique to literary language is also encountered outside literature. As a consequence, what speech-act theorists have taught us about the way words perform outside literature can and should be applied to the particular performance canonically established as literary. "The basic speaker/Audience situation which prevails in a literary work is not fundamentally or uniquely literary. It is not the result of a use of the language different from all other uses. Far from suspending, transforming, or opposing the laws of nonliterary discourse, literature, in this aspect at least, obeys them" (115).

Pratt defends her belief that literature "suspends" nothing at all—a flat contradiction of Searle's belief that authorial pretending suspends normal illocutionary conventions—in several ways. When she applies to literary narration the categories developed to analyze non-literary narration by the sociolinguist William Labov, for instance, modes of understanding developed for language with the highest social charge contribute significantly to apprehending theoretically trans-social discourse. The countless poetic features deployed by ordinary language make the knowledge of literary critics pertinent to non-literary discourse; the traits literature shares with ordinary language make the knowledge of social theorists pertinent to literary criticism. Efforts to wall these two forms of knowledge off from one another are simply misguided.

To use language, a social instrument, is to accept exigent connections with a historical context and the cultural assumptions it conveys. "Literature itself is a speech context. And as with any utterance, the way people produce and understand literary works depends enormously on unspoken, culturally shared knowledge of the rules, conventions and expectations that are in play when language is used in that context" (86). Literary genres furnish Pratt's most persuasive illustration of culture manipulating literary apprehension. We react to a given sentence—"There was a knock at the door" will do—in distinct ways that vary with genre. Knocks on doors aren't the same in detective stories, horror fiction, Harlequin romances, and hard-core pornography, and this spectrum of generic distinctions is directly comparable to the spectrum of illocutionary distinctions available for a non-literary utterance like "the window's open." "There was a knock at the door" puzzles, frightens, thrills, or titillates not in itself but through its generic matrix. In literary as in non-literary discourse, communal procedures are paramount.

So strong is Pratt's commitment to socializing literature that she comes close to refusing differences of whatever kind between the sociality of a text and that of other linguistic acts. To the reification of the text prominent among poetic language theorists, Pratt opposes a subordination of the text to the person who wrote it, an author fundamentally identical to any other "speaker": "it is the speaker, not the text, who invites and attempts to control this focusing [by the reader] according to his own, not the text's intention" (88). A key principle of poetic-language criticism is that the author vanishes— "the death of the author" is a constant metaphor—when the reader confronts a work. Pratt wants to resuscitate the author by assimilating his or her writing to every other discourse.

Her argument is that, since the producers of non-literary language are obviously situated in a community, and since their communal exchanges entail definite speaker/audience interaction, exactly the same interaction must characterize literature.

> Speaker and Audience are present in the literary speech situation [. . .] they have commitments to one another as they do everywhere else, and those commitments are presupposed by both the creator and the receiver of the work. Far from being autonomous, self-contained, self-motivating, context-free objects which exist independently from the "pragmatic" concerns of "everyday" discourse, literary works take place in a context, and like any other utterance they cannot be described apart from that context. (115)

For me, the two halves of that passage make two kinds of claim. The contention in the second half that a text cannot be described apart from a context is in fact independent of the earlier contention that an author and a speaker are for practical purposes indistinguishable, as are what words do in a text and what they do "everywhere else." One speech-act insight is that, because language performs its users' collective engagement with each other, looking at language means looking at what words are doing with, for, and to human beings. That insight does not, however, force all forms of communication into the model supplied by oral exchanges between two individuals in the same space. That literature does indeed "take place in a context" need not lead to the assumption that its context is the same as those that put speaker and audience in one another's presence.

Pratt's discussion of literary genres provides an excellent model for recognizing textual illocution without collapsing it into face-to-face dialogue. Generic determination of a given sentence's force, though certainly the conventional effect of a conventional procedure, can operate felicitously regardless of whether it has exact analogues in extra-literary language use. While words always perform in collaboration with their users, this collaboration can occur in many different ways. Bringing the author back to life is unnecessary to bringing the text back to the world; if "literature itself is a speech context" (86), we can legitimately seek to understand that context *on its own terms*.

In the first lecture of *How to Do Things with Words*, Austin suggested a point that I believe should guide speech-act criticism: writing is as much an illocution as speech, yet the conventions written illocution performs may not be those of oral illocution. The first four examples of the performative, chosen presumably because they make words' power to do things immediately apparent, include a written "speech" act. Although Austin doesn't develop the point, certainly not as it applies to literature, there are major differences between written and oral illocution in the four originary performatives: a wedding, a bet, a ship christening, and a clause in a will. The spoken examples, "I do," "I bet," "I name this ship," do what they say as they are being said. Instantaneous production of their referents—a marriage, a wager, a ship's name—is in fact what makes the performative so immediately compelling a challenge to representational linguistics. But the other example, "I give and bequeath my watch to my brother," does *not* produce a legacy at the moment of enunciation. The testator's death must ensue for his or her property to be transferred, which means that the performative words will do things in a context different from that in which they were produced. In all four founding examples, as in any performative, social conventions make the words active. But with the bequest, the determinant context is not that prevailing at the moment of utterance. Austin's testamentary example introduces the crucial idea that the social formation defining illocution is not the speaker's but the audience's. In speech, the operative communities are usually the same. In non-literary as well as literary writing, they can be wholly distinct.

Austin's concentration on speech was therefore from the beginning not exclusive, and again critics can learn from the theory despite the theorist's objections. There are clear analogies between the illocutionary identities of a will and a text. Most obviously, "I give and bequeath" performs in the absence of the "I." The death of the author is here not at all metaphoric. Moreover, the performance is felicitous or infelicitous not according to the conventions the author knew but according to those society observes when the will is executed. A social revolution prohibiting legacies of private property above a certain value might well send the watch to the state instead of the brother. "I give and bequeath" would then be void because the foundational requirement, Rule A.1, is no longer met. When language is written rather than spoken, when it is literature in the etymological sense that it consists of *letters*, the speaker-hearer model breaks down even though speech-act theory does not.

Model and theory also have separate fates when the language is literary in the institutional sense. As with a testator's words, interaction between language and society has no need for the author's living and breathing self. The face-to-face model, what deconstructionists call the "logocentric" vision of language as fully itself only when spoken, is certainly the major source of speech-act illustrations. But there's no reason whatever to take illustrative material's oral bias to imply theoretical dependence on physical presence. Both a will and a text exercise conventional power through conventional means, both interact with readers in the absence of an author, neither depends on physical presence for its words to perform.

That's why critics are mistaken when they try to contest the validity of a speech-act approach to literature out of the belief that a text's transcendence of presence makes it unavailable for Austinian understanding. Presence is not conventional, Austinian philosophy is wholly conventional. The twists necessary to get from the fact that some performatives are oral to the conviction that literature can't be performative are patent in this refusal of Austinian criticism: "Without a 'real' natural context (although one determined by convention) to guarantee a 'serious' speaker and to ensure a desired response, illocutionary force, in literature, becomes merely an empty, impotent abstraction. Illocutionary acts are those which lose their meaning in representation" (Bauerlein 1986; p. 12). The parenthetical remark that the natural context is determined by convention is as telling as Benveniste's insertion of society into his purely linguistic definition of the performative. What is a real, natural context that's also determined by convention? By definition, conventions are the *opposite* of nature. Illocutionary acts don't lose but *acquire* their meaning in representation. Their force is always representative of the collective identity they perform, and the performance of literature in the contemporary West is poles apart from an "empty, impotent abstraction."

Austin's invention was not *speaker*-act theory but *speech*-act theory. The speaker's absence when a will (or a contract, or a declaration of war) does things is enough to show that speakers' presence when other performatives do something is *coincidental*. Every one of the illustrations habitually put forth to make the performative palpable could retain its exemplary value without a speaker. We can get married by proxy, make a bet with computer blips, suspend the constitution on a printing press, baptize a ship in a registry-office filing cabinet, make a promise in a memo. What matters isn't who produces the words where but what the words do how: not individuals but conventions. Illocutionary force inevitably—constitutively—derives from collective protocols; by definition, a collectivity cannot be reduced to one of its members. Every speech act is an institutional fact; none requires the brute fact of a particular person's presence in a particular place.

What words do depends not on speakers but on (conventional) context. Inside and outside literature, the speaker's physical presence is an illocutionary irrelevancy. What matters are the conventions enacted by his or her speech.

Since the performative can do without the speaker altogether, it can obviously do without the speaker's intentions. Austin made this point fundamental when, again in his first lecture, he attacked what he called the "quite mistaken" view that words are "uttered as (merely) the outward and visible sign, for convenience or other record or for information, of an inward and spiritual act" (Austin 1962; p. 9). We'd have trouble coming up with a better short summary of the intentionalist vision of literary analysis than that. Many critics also devote themselves to seeking the author's inward and spiritual act of which his or her text is an outward and visible sign that has its meaning elsewhere.

Austin insists that this "quite mistaken" project is not only extraneous but also seriously inimical to speech-act theory. Your words implant you in society no matter how much your inner voice says you're not a social creature. Austin was adamant that the force of promises and bets commits even liars and welshers; by the same reasoning, the force of a literary work is independent of its creator's inner disposition. What a text does is no more a matter of personal and individual will than what a marriage does.

Once this is recognized, objections to the concept of poetic language become less its categorization of the text than its failure to see that this is indeed a categorization, one which stands or falls through collective accord or dismissal. To understand the text as autonomous, self-generating, autotelic, self-referential, or any of the other fashionable *self-* and *auto-* compounds is not a discovery but an invention. Because it took hold the same way any locution becomes illocutionary, the Poetic Language Fallacy is better understood as the Poetic Language Convention.

The means through which the convention attained hegemony demonstrate that poetic language is identical to illocutionary force in being a social construct rather than a trans-social quality. Textual autonomy comes from Prague, Moscow, Geneva, and Paris, where it became a fact through the standard procedures applicable to all institutional facts acquiring communal substance. Meetings, journals, articles, books, talks, university courses established the necessary constitutive rules which, when accepted by a large enough number, did indeed constitute the text as TEXT.

In the United States, the social process of constitution was helped along enormously by the affinities between the ideas institutionalized as poetic language and those that had already performed the validity of the New Criticism. Entire departments of great universities went to work to give a European development North American credentials, and they succeeded. That poetic language is now a reality is the effect of a speeded-up, and thus more obvious, version of the same social praxis that has made bets and apologies a reality. All supposedly constative assertions of what the text is were actually happy performatives that made the text what they said.

And a central tenet of speech-act theory is that the question of truth or falsity is irrelevant when a performative succeeds. As Stanley Fish has argued, the vital factor is not an interpretation's inherent validity but its attachment to the community accepting it; in certain contexts the communal connections of textual autonomy are rock-solid. Poetic language may be a fallacy, but it is also an undeniable fact of life for every Western student of literature in the late twentieth century.

This does not of course condemn speech-act criticism to silence. Poetic language too operates as an illocutionary force. Those who analyze it participate in a communal activity—a performance—as surely as those who invented it. Even the TEXT is subject to Rule A.1. However we understand it, our understanding is the conventional effect of a conventional procedure.

Ross Chambers has suggested an excellent model for appreciating the text as text while still recognizing that "text as text" belongs among the performative words that produce what they name. After regretting the tendency of some speech-act critics to concentrate their efforts on literature's incorporation of explicit performatives, on the sort of thing Austin quickly left behind, Chambers suggests a broader model for the illocutionary status of a work of art.

> The "performative" underlying aesthetic discourse could then be something like "I offer myself for interpretation" or "I invite you to interpret me"—supposing, however, that such a speech act can be attributed to the message itself (become its own sender) and that the receiver here designated by "you" can be conceived as a perfectly indeterminate *whom it may concern*. (1980; p. 403, my translation)

Samuel Levin (1976) proposed an analogously global aesthetic performative when he suggested that the sentence underlying every poem was something like "I imagine myself in and invite you to conceive a world in which" followed by the poem. Whereas Chambers and Levin both posit the aesthetic performative as "I invite," however, Levin attributes it to the author, Chambers to the work. Chambers's way is far more Austinian. An aesthetic performative produced by the message rather than the author foregrounds the fact that the forces making literary words do things for readers must be part of the reading, not the writing, experience.

While the receiver of the aesthetic message is for Chambers "perfectly indeterminate" from and for the message, he or she will of necessity receive the message within the perfectly determinate setting Fish calls an interpretive community. That community's conventions will organize the analytic procedures for which the text offers itself in each of its actualizations, and Austin provides invaluable lessons on those procedures in action.

Paul Ricoeur (1981a) has proposed using the text's availability for multiple understandings as a model for apprehending human action in general. What we do as well as what we write is subject to different hermeneutic operations that produce different meanings as circumstances and conventions develop in time. Ricoeur's analogy also works in the other direction. To see the text as act, which an Austinian approach requires, does not at all force us to construe it as an act with one and only one sense. Like the illocutionary force of a given locution, the meaning of a given text derives from the protocols applied to it. Even more than an uncontextualized sentence like "The window's open," the text offers itself for a broad spectrum of conventional identities.

Conventional, not intentional identities. The contrast is even more important for textual illocution than for other kinds, for the intentional fallacy is a crippling handicap in the critical enterprise. It's vital to my belief that Austin has something to say to students of literature that the fallacy not contaminate speech-act theory as a whole. Textual illocution cannot be a serious category if illocutionary force depends on authorial intention. Things are bad enough when Austin denies that his ideas apply to literature. If the nature of those ideas means that we must always pass through the author, speech-act theory doesn't enrich but prevents interesting literary interpretations.

With the stakes so high, I want to go slowly through the steps by which Austin separates the conventions essential to speech acts from the intentions incidental to them. Austin's many allusions to intentionality never take on the meaning Searle draws. When Austin addresses illocution, he subordinates the personal to the social. The illocutionary "act is constituted not by intention or by fact, essentially but by *convention*" (Austin 1962; p. 128). The emphasis is Austin's, but literary critics should make it theirs as well.

The most consequential appearance of intentionality in *How to Do Things with Words* comes while Austin is giving his six rules for performative felicity. The last two of the six require that speakers intend to behave in a certain way and subsequently so behave; out of context, these two rules can indeed make it seem that intention matters, and quite seriously. *In* context, however, intention is as trivial to illocutionary identity as is perlocutionary behavior. Whether we lose a bet and don't pay or make a bet with no intention of paying, we've still made a bet.

How to Do Things with Words therefore draws a stark dividing line between the first four rules for speech acts, those Austin labels A and B and invokes to specify that a conventional procedure must exist and be correctly applied, and the last two, which he labels with the Greek letter Γ and uses to introduce speaker's intentions and behavior. The first four *alone* produce the illocutionary act; the last two simply mean that the act is subject to abuse. As Austin saw, the distinction's a biggie.

> The first big distinction is between all the four rules A and B taken together, as opposed to the two rules Γ (hence the use of Roman as opposed to Greek letters). If we offend against any of the former rules (A's or B's) [...] then the act in question, e.g. marrying, is not successfully performed at all, does not come off, is not achieved. Whereas in the two Γ cases the act *is* achieved. (15–16)

The tripled negation and the italicized affirmation are clear enough. When there is no social convention or the convention is incorrectly applied, the speech act is not performed at all, does not come off, is not achieved. But if the (collective) convention is applied and the only problem is (individual) intention or behavior, then the speech act *is* performed, *does* come off, *is* achieved. The "big distinction" between social and individual requirements for illocution is the big distinction between Austin and Searle.

Some of the sections of Austin's writings that allude to intentions, inner thoughts, and sincerity have already been quoted here. As an example, take this argument that statements go wrong in the same way as promises.

> Suppose I did say "the cat is on the mat" when it is not the case that I believe that the cat is on the mat, what should we say? Clearly it is a case of *insincerity*. In other words: the unhappiness here is, though affecting a statement, exactly the same as the unhappiness infecting "I promise. . ." when I do not intend, do not believe, &c. The insincerity of an assertion is the same as the insincerity of a promise, since both promising and asserting are procedures intended for use by persons having certain thoughts. (Austin 1962; p. 50)

All such statements have to be related to the distinction between *performing* an illocutionary act and *abusing* it. Like promises, assertions entail accepting certain communal conventions. Violating these conventions doesn't abrogate them but sets the speaker outside the community where they operate, as the Boy Who Cried Wolf learned too late. Speech acts count as what a collectivity determines, and their only constitutive rules are those Austin labeled A and B. Rules about individual intention and behavior are at most regulative. (Incidentally, it should be noted that, even in the long consideration of sincerity above, it's the community that decides what thoughts the speaker should have.)

Austin prepares his first lecture's sharp differentiation between constitutive and incidental rules for the performative by refusing every effort to bring inner states into an area where they have no business. When it comes to the things words do, we are quite mistaken to concern ourselves in any way with what's happening inside while language is performing outside. Austin's illustration is the promise, that classic performative which, like the text, takes force not from an individual but from a convention. Austin ridicules the idea that mental reservations can abrogate spoken commitments; before the argument Euripides attributes to Hippolytus, the position that we aren't responsible for what our tongue says if our heart keeps silent, Austin is pitiless: "he *does* promise; the promise here is not even *void*, though it is given *in bad faith*" (11). Even though performatives are most obviously felicitous when intention and convention mesh, in the event of a conflict convention *always* prevails.

The predicatory fervor of this passage memorably expresses Austin's biting contempt for those who set intention first.

> For one who says "promising is not merely a matter of uttering words! It is an inward and spiritual act!" is apt to appear as a solid moralist standing out against a generation of superficial theorizers: we see him as he sees himself, surveying the invisible depths of ethical space, with all the distinction of a specialist in the *sui generis*. Yet he provides Hippolytus with a let-out, the bigamist with an excuse for his "I do" and the welsher with a defence for his "I bet." Accuracy and morality alike are on the side of the plain saying that *our word is our bond*. (10)

Again it's easy to see here a foreshadowing of current debates pitting those who believe in the normative function of the Author's "inward and spiritual" intention against the "generation of superficial theorizers" who valorize the text as act. Austin unmistakably aligns himself with the theorizers. Words bind because of their *social* validation as acts, and no *individual* feeling or thought can make them void.

Since Austin sometimes takes it for granted that he doesn't need to repeat points he's already made clear, some of his references to inward states don't subordinate them to social conventions as categorically as others. It's therefore comprehensible that his decontextualized references to intention have been misunderstood. What I find completely incomprehensible is that readers have even taken Austin's fire-and-brimstone dismissal of the inner self to mean exactly the opposite of what it so passionately says. One example: "Austin recognizes this fact at least indirectly by laying emphasis on sincerity as the main condition for a successful linguistic action: *our word is our bond*" (Iser 1975; pp. 12–13). A passage arguing with unusual intensity that sincerity is irrelevant is cited to prove it's essential. Accusations that speech-act theory relies on intentionalism have little to do with Austin, much to do with those who have misread him.

With the author's intentions inoperative, textual illocution is exactly the same as oral illocution with the speaker's intentions unperformative. For literary and non-literary illocution alike, what speech-act theory addresses is language's participation, its dynamic and productive participation, in the processes of collective life. Or rather, speech-act theory reveals that language is *among* the processes of collective life, which are in turn *inside* language. This interpenetration, vital to the force of a literary work, means that speech-act critics will interpret just like Austin, by attending to the communal identity required for a conventional procedure to have conventional effect.

Ohmann and Pratt agree with one another on the necessity for this attention, but they direct it to different communities. Pratt's deep concern to keep the text socially active leads her to keep the author alive and take the speaker/hearer model as analytic paradigm. Ohmann's recognition that the speaker/hearer model breaks down leads him to concentrate on the text's interaction with the social being of its readers. We can perfectly well learn from both and agree with Pratt that the text was indeed doing the world's business when it appeared and with Ohmann that it continues to interact with the world's business as long as it has readers.

If we do so agree, then speech-act criticism has both an interpretive and a reader-response branch. Each looks at language as performance rather than description, each understands that language can become performance only in collaboration with society. Neither branch requires undoing the discoveries of formal literary analysis any more than speech-act theory itself requires undoing the discoveries of formal linguistics. For *textual* illocution as well, what language does matters incomparably more than what it is. Speech-act criticism of textual doing can coexist quite comfortably with scholars willing to stop when they've identified a feature of textual being.

6

Performing the Performative

In practical criticism with a speech-act orientation, pride of place is held by drama. A theatrical spectator's experience begins and ends with observation of words doing things; dramatic force and illocutionary force are one whenever a play is performed. To borrow Richard Ohmann's metaphor, "in a play, the action rides on a train of illocutions" (1973; p. 83). When spectators get on the train, they're carried deep into the human interaction that gives stage presence to characters and subject matter to speech-act theorists.

For Ross Chambers, understanding the theater and understanding illocution are mutually invigorating versions of a single epistemological undertaking. As a result, the speech act "appears as the theatrical act *par excellence* [. . .] the fundamental subject of dramatic narration is the illocutionary relationship [. . .] the special vocation of the theater is to explore the consequences of this intuition that 'doing is saying' and 'saying is doing'" (1980; pp. 401–402, my translation). The theater's special capacity to make clear that saying is doing manifests an identity that functions in a no less decisive but sometimes less apparent manner in everyday life. The words of its characters perform a play as the words of its members perform a society.

The illocutionary relationship Chambers sees as drama's fundamental subject is, on its surface as in its depths, collective. What Ohmann says about illocution in general also applies to its theatrical representation. "The indicator or indicators of illocutionary force implant the meaning in the stream of social interaction; they are what make speech take hold, and what make language more than the medium of information exchange that philosophers and linguists long seem to have thought it" (1972b; p. 118). Theater too contests the descriptive fallacy's definition of language as a means of saying things. To fulfill the responsibility drama assigns it, language must also do things with direct and perceptible impact on its characters, "implanted in the stream of social interaction" as an unavoidable consequence of implantation in the stream of theatrical narration. Austin was well advised to appropriate the lexicon of the theater—*perform, act*—as the core of his terminology.

Given the collective nature of illocution, there may well be a reason for speech-act critics' attraction to the theater besides the prominence dramatic performances establish for linguistic performatives. Drama more palpably involves collective experience than other Western genres. We read most texts alone, we attend theatrical texts with the rest of the audience. Behind most texts is a single author, within the theatrical text is a troupe. Dramatic practice and speech-act theory accord equal emphasis to the communal nature of human experience, and the theater's prominence in speech-act criticism is suited to its embodiment of the speech-act vision of the world.

Keir Elam's *The Semiotics of Theatre and Drama* uses the speech-act vision to contest the distinction between a play's action and its dialogue. In Elam's view, dialogue *constitutes* action, and we must apprehend everything characters say as "speech events" with the same executive power Austin assigns speech acts. "The speech event is, in its own right, the chief form of interaction in the drama" (1980; p. 157). Stage language continuously refutes the idea that linguistic expression depicts rather than produces.

Elam draws essential principles for theatrical criticism from Austin's insight into the speech act's communal production.

> It is this social, interpersonal, executive power of language, the pragmatic "doing things with words," which is dominant in the drama. Dramatic discourse is a network of complementary and conflicting illocutions and perlocutions: in a word, linguistic *interaction*, not so much descriptive as performative. Whatever its stylistic, poetic and general "aesthetic" function, the dialogue is in the first place a mode of *praxis* which sets in opposition the different personal, social and ethical forces of the dramatic world. (159)

Praxis and *lexis*, action and language, performance and representation, all the paired terms opposing what humans say and what they do come together in the theater as in Austin.

Elam introduces a wealth of theatrical examples to prove the importance of illocutionary identity to dramatic dialogue through the ages. He also proposes a complicated but comprehensive system of notation enabling him to schematize the relationships between illocution and a play's other components, a schema persuasively applied to the opening lines of *Hamlet*. Throughout the dramatic excerpts he addresses, Elam's primary concern remains how drama's "personal, social and ethical forces" acquire their concrete presence by dialogue's "social, interpersonal, executive power."

One of Elam's examples is a long extract from Act V, Scene iv of Marlowe's *Edward II*. The scene leads up to Mortimer's beheading of Kent despite the attempt made by the young prince Edward III to save the man who is also his uncle. Elam highlights the number and importance of the scene's explicit performatives, the language that, as in Kent's "I defy thee!" to Mortimer, makes verbalization and enactment of mortal conflict a single process. Stage directions are superfluous, what characters do proceeds immediately from what they say. "I defy thee" has the classic performative traits of "I promise," and its dramatic impact in Marlowe exemplifies why Austin decided that the things words do deserved more respect than the things they say.

Elam also addresses how characters' social situation becomes manifest in the illocutionary possibilities open to them, another demonstration that explicitly performative verbs have special power to convey the combination of the linguistic and extra-linguistic that constitutes communal existence. The young Edward III is theoretically God's elected, a monarch whose word should be law. But Mortimer has usurped royal authority, and the illocutionary stance of a ruler is grotesque in a supplicant. Despite his birth, Edward cannot felicitously command but must abjectly beg when he speaks for and of his uncle. "And yet methinks I should *command*/But, seeing I cannot, I'll *entreat* for him." The illocutionary gulf between commanding and entreating is also the sociopolitical gulf between ruling and being deposed. What words do or fail to do *effects* who Marlowe's characters are or fail to be.

The most dangerous temptation facing speech-act criticism is to take for granted Austin's insights into the active presence of social praxis in the illocutionary lexicon. Because we have learned from a master that the stuff of existence adheres to the choice between words like *entreat* and *command*, we sometimes neglect to explain why we find those choices of inexhaustible interest. When we leave our knowledge of the doing in words implicit, we can sound silly to those for whom words' function is still primarily saying. The most frequent complaint directed at speech-act criticism is that it produces more lists than explanation. It's always incumbent on us to make clear why our lists are worth compiling.

Among the attractive features of Elam's illocutionary approach to the theater is his determined resistance to the enticements of assemblage. Fully alert to the intersections between verbal action and other kinds, he highlights not only the language but also the praxis of sentences like "I defy thee." Nevertheless, he fails to capitalize on one important method of keeping social relations ahead of lexical inventories, the speech-act vision of the constative as no less dependent on Rule A.1 than the performative.

The punch of speech-act criticism comes less from sensitivity to *certain* kinds of language than from recognition that *all* kinds of language make tangible the network of relationships and agreements in which humans and their signs are always embedded. Whether applied to literary or ordinary language, a speech-act understanding is dense with the commitments and determinants producing the identity of speakers along with the force of speech. As it happens, the scene from *Edward II* that Elam used to demonstrate the dramatic stature of performative speech displays equally well the social force of constative speech. Marlowe's dialogue performs collective production of truth as well as collective delimitation of felicity.

When brought before the usurper Mortimer, the captive Kent defends himself for trying to save King Edward II by producing the simplest constative structures the English language can provide. His plain saying is suited to his plain certainty that what he did was incontestably correct.

> Mortimer: Did you attempt his rescue, Edmund? Speak.
> Kent: Mortimer, I did; he is our king.

Kent's direct statement of agency—again, to be more direct than "I did" requires a language other than English—is justified by an equally direct statement of identity, "he is our king." But Kent's language assumes that identity is referential rather than constative, that it proceeds from the nature of reality rather than from collectively observed conventional procedures. *Constative* existence as king is not the result of God's will but of the will performed by those within a kingdom. If "x" is a political function, then "he is our x" is true or false solely through the agreements holding among those who make "our" plural. Kent's act will be punished by death because the community within which he is now speaking, the community newly established by Mortimer, recognizes Kent's semantics no more than his authority.

That constative and performative must succeed or fail together, that their success or failure derives exclusively from communal action, is poignant in this conflict over Kent's own identity.

> Edward III: My lord, he is my uncle, and shall live.
> Mortimer: My lord, he is your enemy, and shall die.

Again the "he is x" pattern, this time in parallel utterances, embodies the necessity for collective ratification for any statement of identity to be felicitous. This time the mortal stakes of constative identification are foregrounded by the dual nomenclature's development into the dual conclusion "shall live/shall die." The performative force of third-person *shall* as an expression of the speaker's determination was far stronger in Elizabethan English than in today's, and the parallelism of Marlowe's text consequently exemplifies the *common* dependence of constative and performative success on group dynamics. Collective conditions oppose the two occurrences of constative *is* as directly as the two occurrences of performative *shall*. The play dramatizes what Kent "is" not as a brute fact but as an institutional fact, and for the present the institutions that count belong to Mortimer.

The scene's conclusion repeats its demonstration that collective interaction gives all language whatever expressive value it possesses. Mortimer follows up on his statement to Prince Edward that Kent must die with a reiterated command to his soldiers to bring the death about. The collective circumstances making the command perform also make the statement accurate. Mortimer to Edward III and then to his troops:

> 'Tis for your highness' good, and for the realm's.
> How often shall I bid you bear him hence?

As Mortimer's command is obeyed and he is being led away to die, Kent almost sees that illocutionary force applies to what is as well as to what is bid. Though still below full awareness that royal identity is no more than a communal performance, Kent at least asks Mortimer two questions that show him to be far less certain that it's a divine gift: "Art thou king? Must I die at thy command?" Kent's second question explicitly addresses performative force, "at thy *command*." His strategy was to show that the answer to this question must be negative because there could only be a negative answer to his first question of constative fact, "Art thou king?" While he was absolutely right to think that his two questions were really just one, his (fatal) error was not seeing that both questions addressed communal accord instead of transcendent truth. Because Mortimer could issue royal commands, he acquired royal identity as well.

And he drives the point home when he answers Kent's second question in a form that also answers the first. "Must I die at thy command?" uses the contemptuous second-person singular *thy*. Mortimer responds with the first-person plural of the royal *we*, which he then instantly justifies by another performative exercise of the royal prerogative to issue a felicitous order. "At our command. Once more, away with him." The thought-provoking quantity of sociopolitical messages in that little word *our* makes it an apt conclusion to Marlowe's demonstration that constative and performative language must necessarily perform and signify, act and state, in tandem.

The scandal isn't just that Mortimer is obeyed and Edward III is not. Because the concept of felicity designates a conventional position rather than a perlocutionary result, for the usurper to command felicitously means much more than that people do what he says. He and his comrades have done nothing less than deprive God's agents of agency, and their language speaks a whole new world. The *acts* they commit might only be an insurrection, the *speech acts* make it a revolution. Kent's last questions come from his bewildered sensation that the reality he knows should but doesn't prohibit the language he hears.

The dialogue and characters on stage coalesce in a series of memorable insights not only into the number of things words effectively do but also into the social ground of what they accurately say. The passage Elam chose for its concern with the performative in action turns out to be no less rich in felicitously productive constatives. Marlowe represents the seizure of political power as so profoundly affecting the world that the rules for saying what is are as much up for grabs as those for commanding what is to be. With obsessive regularity, the play alternates between new performative conventions and new constative truths. Like Austin, Marlowe was keenly aware that suprasocial description was always fallacious.

Marlowe continues his own exposition of the point by showing his audience what the "legitimate" king Edward II has been about while Mortimer is stealing his kingdom, his wife, and his son. According to Renaissance thought, no constative should be more reliable than that the king is king. In Marlowe's tragedy, no constative has more need of communal performance. The king is on his throne only so long as subjects keep him there; if subjects abrogate the conventional procedures of which royalty is a conventional effect, the king is literally as well as figuratively in deep shit.

> This dungeon where they keep me is the sink
> Wherein the filth of all the castle falls.
> [. . .] And there in mire and puddle have I stood
> This ten days' space.

In *Shakespeare's Universe of Discourse* (1984), Elam makes productive use of Austin for analysis of a less lugubrious topic, Shakespearean comedy. Here a crucial reference is to Austin's insistence—a necessary consequence of the fact that illocution is never unilateral—that words doing things require an effect on the audience as well as an utterance by the speaker. Much of comedy, including but by no means limited to its Shakespearean version, relies heavily on the breakdown of what Austin calls audience uptake. Misunderstandings, radical discontinuities between what speakers and hearers think words are doing, have figured prominently in comedy from the Greeks to the present. Given the mutually constitutive nature of communal protocols and illocutionary force, such breakdowns are vital in comedy's ability to incorporate a social vision into its laughable plots. When, in Elam's terms, the effect of a (non)dialogue is "not so much illocutionary as dislocationary" (1984; p. 211), spectators experience to the full the replacement of the old by the new vital to the comic spirit. Communicative collapse is often the mark of social transformation, and comedy's delight in illocutionary failures is part of its commitment to figuring renewal of a failed society.

Elias Rivers and his collaborators have analyzed the Spanish theater's display of the affinities between dramatic and illocutionary performance. With Myra Gann, Rivers has, for instance, explored the performative devastation wrought by the apparently constative utterance "You lie" in classic Spanish theater. It's doubtful that world literature furnishes a more explosive instance of constative-performative interpenetration and of language's coordination with social norms than the things Spain's Golden Age dramatists represent "You lie" as doing. "Explosive" is the right word. Within the code of nobility as depicted in Spanish theater, "You lie" blasts to bits all the endowments and achievements assembled in a man of honor. Utterance of this insult suffices to take away all merit, instantly and irresistibly. A lifetime of valiant acts can vanish before the onslaught of this tiny bit of speech. Truth value—whether the person addressed is or isn't lying—is absolutely irrelevant to the all-destroying performance of "You lie." Identity is a communal rather than individual creation in Spanish theater of the Golden Age, and if a felicitous "You lie" enters communal discourse identity as a man of honor dissipates at once.

In her study of Calderón's *Secret Vengeance for Secret Insult,* Gann adumbrates some of the felicity conditions applying to "You lie." Speaker and hearer must both be noble and male, for example. Correctness is totally without impact on felicity, for like any classic performative the insult in Calderón bears its truth within itself. It "allows one man to destroy another by means of a verbal formula which is not subject to any true-false verification" (Gann 1986; p. 39). Saying is doing with no appeal, characters "find themselves faced with the danger of having a dishonor *voiced* and therefore constituted" (42).

Calderón's characters, fully conscious of the performative essence of human speech, impotently contrast the force of speech acts to the impotence of every other kind. "Oh vile law of the world! That just or unjust words can stain the proud honor acquired over so many years, that the old reputation as honorable man can lie flat, cut down by the scythe of a voice!" (quoted, Gann 1986; p. 41, my translation).

The voice-as-scythe cuts to the quick no matter whose voice it is. Gann emphasizes that what disparaging words do in Calderón is so overpowering that *whoever* utters them must be put to death. Even though the words not the speaker do the damage, only the speaker can be held accountable for the damage done. I must therefore retaliate against the insult without regard for my feelings toward its source. No personal relationship can prevail against the *absolute* power of social discourse.

Suppose my close friend heard someone insult me and repeated the offensive words in my presence; I would have to kill the friend, for the words destroy me in themselves, regardless of how my friend intended them. The logical conclusion is that suicide is my only recourse if I attack my own honor out loud: "I call God to witness that, if I said it to myself, I would put myself to death; and I am my own best friend" (quoted; p. 47, my translation).

As more than one teacher of Spanish literature has experienced first-hand, Calderón's honor plays evoke more snickering than catharsis in twentieth-century America. There is undeniably much that's ridiculous in a character pledging to kill himself if he ever accuses himself of lying, and I had serious reservations about bringing the vicissitudes of honor among Golden Age hidalgos into this survey of speech-act theory's contributions to contemporary criticism.

I decided to do so because the very exaggeration in the speech-act vision of the world in Calderón's *Secret Vengeance for Secret Insult* makes it easier to see points also valid in the vision's less extreme formulations. Calderón makes it blindingly apparent that what words do isn't the creation of the *individual* who speaks them. What performs is the words' interaction with a *social* order, dramatized as so overwhelming that I must kill everyone, myself included, who produces words from which the wrong kind of interaction takes off. Intention, good or ill will, and all the other features of personal subjectivity are completely inoperative here, and the fact that they remain operative elsewhere doesn't prevent their subordination to the collective conventions Calderón depicts as *uniquely* performative.

Analogously, the universal recognition among Calderón's characters that it's inane to fret over the truth value of the formally constative "You lie" is pertinent to social circumstances in which truth value
is by convention considered the constative's prime felicity condition.
To use the scholarly example once more, an utterance like "His work is
derivative and banal" that circulates among the academic community
does things with no more dependence on descriptive validity than
required for "You lie" in Golden Age Spain. Calderón's theater is a
speech-act exemplum because our alienation from the conventions
lived by its characters makes it easier to recognize the essential traits
of the conventions we ourselves live.

In his *Quixotic Scriptures*, Elias Rivers addresses the classic Spanish
theater's vision of another convention with continuing contemporary
relevance, the comparative illocutionary force of spoken and written
performatives. In an assessment relevant to the illocutionary energy
in Marlowe's *Edward II*, Rivers contends that "the theater of Golden
Age Spain, like that of Elizabethan England, provided a sociolinguistic laboratory within which to test old and new ideas about the authority of speech acts" (87). One experiment in the laboratory was performed in an anonymous play called *Estrella of Seville*, which for
Rivers stages the threat writing poses to the conventions a society has
traditionally performed orally.

While several incidents and conversations in the play represent
writing's dangers, the most direct expression of speech's superiority
comes when a character tears up a written promise from his king and
gives this explanation:

> I'm amazed that your royal Majesty has such a low opinion of me.
> Documents and papers for me! Treat me more simply, for my nobility
> has greater trust in you than in paper. If your words have the power
> to move mountains, if they perform everything they say (*cuanto dicen
> obran*), and if you here give me your word, there is, sire, no need for
> papers [. . .] paper in fact partially discredits your word. (*He tears
> it up*) (quoted, Rivers 1983; p. 85)

Calderón violently severed language's performative power from its
speaker; with comparable violence, *Estrella of Seville* cuts illocutionary force away from purely linguistic identity. The *same* words from
the *same* source can either move mountains and perform everything
they say or become a contemptible piece of trash to be torn up and
thrown away. Again the things words do are understandable solely
through the attitude toward them assumed and enacted by a collectivity. Look just at the words and you have no way whatever of knowing

what they're doing; communal opinion can make their written production contemptible, their oral production omnipotent.

Stanley Fish buttressed Rivers's view that Elizabethan England joined Golden Age Spain in making theater a speech-act laboratory through discussion of Shakespeare's *Coriolanus* in his "How to Do Things with Austin and Searle." Fish's essay is both an admirable demonstration of the intellectual gains made by framing interpretation in speech-act categories and an important theoretical statement. Both its practical and theoretical arguments have had prodigious impact, and I address them in turn.

Fish sees *Coriolanus* as "a speech-act play" (Fish 1980; pp. 221, 244), one in which "it is almost as if [the characters] were early practitioners of Oxford or 'ordinary language' philosophy" (221). The drama revolves around, and is resolved by, the multilateral bonds accepted willy-nilly by every member of a society, all of whom must affirm the bonds in the illocutionary speech they continuously and necessarily produce. Because Coriolanus sees himself as a man of such surpassingly self-sufficient merit that bonds to others are an affront, he systematically perverts and distorts his illocutionary stances. When he seeks to become consul, the constitutive rules for his candidacy require that he request the votes of his fellow citizens in the warranted ways. Convinced that his fitness for the consulship is self-evident, however, Coriolanus asks for votes in such a contemptuous manner that his illocutions do not confirm but refuse membership in a collectivity. The speech acts that should manifest community obliterate it instead.

Calderón's characters are so sensitive to the power of social discourse that they see a felicitous insult as wiping out a lifetime of noble deeds. Coriolanus is so blind to the power of social discourse that he believes his lifetime of noble deeds has set him above and beyond connection to other people. He therefore requests support without making the request active, and the tragedy that results repeats the lesson of *Estrella of Seville*: words count not in themselves but solely in function of their social apprehension.

When Coriolanus brings himself to utter the language of request— "I pray," "I request you," "I do beseech you"—he also emits clear signals that he is spitting on those he's talking to. Social discourse therefore sets him outside itself as he has set himself outside it. "He mocked us when he begged our voices [. . .] He flouted us downright [. . .] He used us scornfully." The opposition is between "us" and "I," a community and an ego. Because illocutionary force is always communal, Coriolanus cannot exercise it when he is also performing himself as apart and alone. Fish: "Coriolanus's every illocutionary gesture is one that declares his disinclination to implicate himself in the reciprocal web of obligations that is the content of the system of conventional speech acts. To put it simply, Coriolanus is always doing things (with words) to set himself apart" (213). Speech performs only through group dynamics; to repudiate the group is to abandon the performative.

At least the performative as that group has instituted it. Coriolanus goes so far as to set himself up as a one-man collectivity in which his own procedures have at least as much executive power as Rome's. His simultaneous rejection and replacement of Rome's verbal performances is sensational when he responds to banishment from the state by hurling back at the state a defiant "I banish you." Fish calls this counter-banishment the "most spectacular illocutionary act performed in *Coriolanus*" (213) because of its comprehensive subversion/inversion of all the group-group member relationships normally enacted through verbal communication. Coriolanus not only sets himself outside the state, he sets himself in its place; the system of constitutive rules required for his "I banish you" to be felicitous undermines each of the constitutive rules by which Rome maintains itself as Rome.

Fish structures his reading of the Rome-Coriolanus nexus around Searle's writings as well as Austin's, and the points he takes from the two speech-act theorists suggest an answer to the question implicit in Fish's title. How do you do things with Austin and Searle? By making full use of Searle's work when it follows Austin's and rejecting it when it deviates. Searle's taxonomy of illocutions is essential to Fish's analysis of the crushing impact of the things done and not done by Coriolanus's words and silences. The schema in Searle's *Speech Acts*, for example, makes it clear that the act of greeting has unique status among performatives. Whereas all illocutions, which is to say all utterances, perform the speaker's participation in collective existence, greetings alone have performance of sociability as their *sole* reason for being. We promise to do x, we bet that y, we protest against z; in greeting, we just greet. Fish can therefore understand Coriolanus's "I banish you" as nothing more than an anti-climactic follow-up to his earlier resolve not to greet his fellow Romans, not to let "Good Morrow" pass his lips. The propositional content of all other speech acts can conceal their performance of communal ties and delude us into believing we are saying things but doing nothing. The absence of propositional content in a greeting makes the delusion impossible. Coriolanus's renunciation of sociable speech signals his withdrawal from social existence.

Despite Fish's productive and provocative use of Searle's schemas, he decisively repudiates Searle's concern for intentionality. Fish accords capital importance to the fact that Coriolanus's failure in requesting support can in no way be attributed to mental and emotional reservations, to the *unperformed* inward and spiritual self Austin kicked out of speech-act theory. All that Rome asks is that Coriolanus go through the motions; no one cares how he feels. But he didn't go through the motions, he "did not ask, but mock." His inner state is irrelevant, what matters is the absence of the outer forms for requesting and the presence of forms for insulting: *He flouted us, he mocked us, he used us scornfully.* As his community receives them, Coriolanus's speech acts wouldn't count as requests even were his soul filled to overflowing with love and good will for all Romans.

For Fish, Searle's own insistence on what an utterance "counts as" takes the acts it performs away from the speaker's intentions.

> "Counts as" is the important phrase [. . .] because it gets at the heart of the speech-act position on intention. Intention, in the view of that theory, is a matter of what one takes responsibility for by performing certain conventional (speech) acts. The question of what is going on inside, the question of the "*inward* performance" is simply bypassed; speech-act theory does not rule on it. (203)

In a move of admirable courtesy, Fish cites Searle much more prominently while appropriating his ideas than while contesting them. Nevertheless, the broadly heuristic use Fish makes of some parts of Searle's writing is possible only through categorical refusal of other parts. Intention, which Fish says speech-act theory doesn't rule on, can be for Searle the most important rule of all.

We saw earlier that Fish also distances himself from Searle's view of fiction. His doing so is an important gesture in the theoretical section of "How to Do Things with Austin and Searle," which addresses the priority of a community's interpretive operations over all reified and extra-communal concepts that Fish writes as "Reality, the Real World, Objective Fact" (243). The concept of interpretive communities is invaluable in explaining how a society's constative utterances constitute their own representational validity, and Fish's repudiation of objective Reality is part of his validation of collective reality. The important question becomes not what is but how it is performed, not whether brute facts exist but how institutional facts circulate.

While establishing his priorities, however, Fish sometimes sounds as if words' executive power can be independent of their social matrix. In contesting Richard Ohmann's insistence that speech acts and social interaction are one and the same, for instance, Fish draws a curious distinction between what is "social" and what is "conventional": "in speech-act theory the notion of felicity isn't social but conventional [. . .] The notion of felicity is social only in the narrow sense that it is tied to conditions specified by a society" (225). This narrow sense sounds a lot like a comprehensive sense. If the conventions and conditions specified by a society aren't social, what are they?

When Fish contrasts his narrow sense to "the larger sense that we must wait for social circumstances to *emerge* before [felicity] can be determined" (225), he does more than oppose illocution and perlocution. He also seems to want to separate society's conventional structure from its material shape, the protocols it observes from the circumstances created when its members act. The social/conventional opposition would therefore actually be a material/conventional opposition, and Fish's objection to the word *social* may result from an implicit critical quarrel. Within a certain historicist perspective, all that deserves the label *social* is what Fish capitalizes and dismisses as Reality, the Real World, Objective Fact. Once more, however, speech-act theory displaces the antagonistic terms that organize such critical polemics. Illocution, as much a historical reality as revolution, deserves to have its social core named no matter what sense other critical paradigms establish by their own use of the adjective. Although Fish's sensitivity to words' social function is acute, he tries hard to give it another name.

The objection to his new terminology is that the social/conventional split is strongly reminiscent of Searle's natural/conventional split, and Fish himself persuasively points out that speech-act parameters prohibit any such contrast (243). Those same parameters prohibit identifying the social with the Objective. There are no conventions without humans who observe them, and humans are always socially situated. Illocutionary force is certainly conventional, but *societies* empower conventions to establish illocution as a force.

The combination of awareness that society makes language active with reluctance to call the language social is also apparent in Fish's double definition of what happens in *Coriolanus* after its title character leaves Rome. One component of the definition foregrounds the absurdity of attempts to find what Coriolanus calls "a world elsewhere," a world he believes will allow him to live in radiant, god-like independence. As Fish puts it, "the truth is that there is no world elsewhere, at least not in the sense Coriolanus intends, a world where it is possible to stand freely, unencumbered by obligations and dependencies. There are only other speech-act communities" (218). When Coriolanus carries on his rebellion against Rome by military force, even his spectacular success on the battlefield depends absolutely on the collective ratification necessary to make (his and all) military commands felicitous. Because refusal of one set of conventions is instantaneous insertion in another, Coriolanus's journey away from Rome leads not to Olympus but to another all-too-human state.

Besides exposing the delusion in Coriolanus's wish to transcend social bonds, however, Fish also suggests that existence above society might after all be possible. I'm thinking of how Fish summarizes Coriolanus's military prowess: "He is, in short, exactly what he always wanted to be, a natural force whose movement through the world is independent of all supports except those provided by his own virtue. He is complete and sufficient unto himself. He is a God" (217). Despite the fact that there is no world elsewhere but only other speech-act communities, Coriolanus is here represented as becoming "exactly what he always wanted to be." No longer social but "natural," no longer in a collectivity but wholly self-sufficient, Coriolanus has escaped the human condition and become a God. And as when Searle deflects the speech-act category of declarations by introducing God's "Let there be light," Fish's admission of divinity is refusal of illocution. The Austinian vision of what words do in society becomes a suggestion that they do things all by themselves.

Like his practical criticism, Fish's theoretical commentary assumes an ambiguous attitude toward what makes speech act. The double definition of Coriolanus as communally bound and divinely autonomous has its counterpart in the double definition of language as both requiring and not requiring collective ratification. In this passage, a collectivity seems superfluous.

> It might be objected that to reason in this way is to imply that one can constitute a state simply by declaring it to exist. That of course is exactly what happens: a single man plants a flag on a barren shore and claims everything his eye can see in the name of a distant monarch or for himself; another man, hunted by police and soldiers, seeks refuge in a cave, where, alone or in the company of one or two fellows, he proclaims the birth of a revolutionary government. (216)

That of course is not exactly what happens. If a "single man" or a "man alone" says something, he produces not an illocution but a pure locution, a form of speech that cannot act because it is cut off from the collective forces that make all performatives work. Although declarations of independence figure prominently among the speech acts that unmistakably change the world, they do so only when a mass performs their validity. Fish's revolutionary is cut off from the mass and seems to have the same supernatural (and hence supra-illocutionary) power accorded Coriolanus, "the declarative of divine fiat, the logos, the *all*-creating word" (217).

The logos and the performative are respectively the least and the most human of language forms. While both do what they say, the sources of their power are wholly incommensurable. Where God is, speech-act theory has nothing to say.

Since Fish's interpretation of Shakespeare decisively corrects his suggestion of Coriolanus's divinity, it was to be expected that his conflation of performative and logos is set right as well. The state that in the sketch of a revolutionary and an explorer comes from words nobody hears also depends entirely on audience reaction: "declarative (and other) utterances do not merely mirror or reflect the state; they *are* the state, which increases and wanes as they are or are not taken seriously" (216). Words *are* the state because they are "taken seriously" by their hearers, a collective process that is both another way of characterizing illocutionary force and another way of saying that speech acts because humans interact. Fish's lesson is finally that, for critics as for Coriolanus, there is no world elsewhere.

A final instance of Fish's double positions on illocution: repeated insistence that "*Coriolanus* is a speech-act play" (221, 244) was in the original essay part of a contention that Austinian criticism was appropriate to this text but not to others, that what Fish does with Austin and Searle is not generalizable to other interpretive endeavors. The inherent nature of *Coriolanus* produces a "fit between the play and the theory" (245) that imbues speech-act categories with powerful but sharply limited analytic value. It would be wrong either to deny that *Coriolanus* is about speech acts or to assume that other texts are about the same thing.

In the preface to the essay written several years later, Fish categorically dismisses those earlier assertions. Now what the play is about is a function of the presuppositions with which Fish approached it: "the play as it really is is the play as it appears obviously to be from the perspective of some interpretive system or other. *Coriolanus* is a speech-act play for me because it is with speech-act theory in mind that I approached the play in the first place" (200). Although he himself doesn't draw the conclusion, Fish's revised position invites rather than prohibits critics to interpret other texts "with speech-act theory in mind." The great coherence and drive of Fish's explanation comes not from the unique status of *Coriolanus* but from the vast relevance of *How to Do Things with Words*.

Fish's original warning that speech-act theory has restricted critical relevance is not idiosyncratic. Other essays in speech-act criticism have also combined their demonstration that the theory is fruitful with cautionary announcements that the fruit grows only on their tree. Albert Prince, for instance, uses Fish's original language and argument to make the same point about a different text from a different literature. Because Lope de Vega's *Fuenteovejuna* "is a speech-act play" (Prince 1986; p. 156), Prince admonishes, it would be wrong to believe the method allowing him to analyze Lope can be applied to other authors.

This is a puzzling trope. I can't think of any other school of criticism whose practitioners warn that the school has strictly limited classroom space. On the contrary, most critical movements (structuralism, deconstruction, feminism, Marxism, New Criticism, psychoanalysis; the list could go on) take it as a duty to announce that what they do with a given text can and should be done with an unlimited number of others. Given the widespread strategy of arguing that an analysis is valid here because its principles apply elsewhere as well, why have speech-act critics chosen to say rather that their analysis is valid here because its principles don't apply elsewhere?

I think the answer is that speech-act principles have *such* broad applicability that it can be scary to experience their explanatory power. Critics tend to think there must be something unique to the object of analysis when an analytic method with relatively few practitioners turns out to furnish so efficient a conceptual model. The reasoning might go like this: "It's obvious that speech-act theory has made a huge contribution to my understanding of this work, but why haven't more critics seen the theory's potential? There must be a peculiar conjunction between the work I'm considering and the questions Austin asked." With more and more critics discovering the conjunction, fewer and fewer will need to define it as peculiar.

The theoretical section of Fish's essay accords seemly prominence to the affinities between Austin's thought and the recent recognition among philosophers and literary critics that language has never submitted itself to merely representational duties. Like Austin's own, the work of such influential continental figures as Jacques Lacan, Jacques Derrida, and Friedrich Nietzsche is in unending and unyielding rebellion against the descriptive fallacy's view that language's function is to represent the extra-linguistic world. The frequent assumption of a great divide between the axioms of European and Anglo-American philosophies of language is just wrong.

Shoshana Felman uses the principles common to Austin and contemporary continental thinkers, especially Jacques Lacan, as the basis for her analysis of Molière's *Don Juan* in *The Literary Speech Act: Don Juan with Austin, or Seduction in Two Languages* (1983). Like Fish's essay, Felman's book is both a theoretical situation of speech-act philosophy and a practical demonstration of the philosophy's value for literary interpretation. I again take the two components in turn, this time starting with theory.

The Literary Speech Act argues with enticing persuasiveness for the importance of a side of Austin often neglected, his infectious delight in pointing out the ruses of language and in disposing his own language so that it will *perform* the mischievousness it depicts. *Fun* is a key word in much of Austin's work, and the fun he seems to have writing spills over into the experience we have reading. Felman emphasizes that Austin is funny as well as fun whenever he gets into gear. The monumental importance of *How to Do Things with Words* in deadly serious activities can conceal the lively joke in its title. How-to books are so far beyond the pale of serious literature that the *New York Times* makes them a none-of-the-above category. The *Times* bestseller lists are divided into three parts, "fiction," "nonfiction," and "advice, how-to and miscellaneous." Austin's weightiest contribution to twentieth-century thought has a title that doesn't fit under either the "fiction" or "nonfiction" classifications that ought to include all thought-contributing literature of any kind.

For Felman, the titles of Austin's essays continue the joke. "Three Ways of Spilling Ink," "Unfair to Facts," and "How to Talk—Some Simple Ways" also begin Austin's most serious work on a self-deprecating suggestion that the work is not to be taken seriously. The suggestions permeate the body of the essays as well; Felman provides a long list of examples, from which I take five.

> Suppose I tie a string across a stairhead. A fragile relative, from whom I have expectations, trips over it, falls, and perishes [. . .] Maybe I had better claim I was simply passing the time, playing cat's cradle, practicing tying knots. (Austin 1961; pp. 274–275)

> In philosophy it is *can* in particular that we seem so often to uncover, just when we had thought some problem settled, grinning residually up at us like the frog at the bottom of the beer mug. (231)

> You will have heard it said, I expect, that over-simplification is the occupational disease of philosophers, and in a way one might agree with that. But for a sneaking suspicion that it's their occupation. (252)

> I think we should not despair too easily and talk, as people are apt to do, about the *infinite* uses of language. Philosophers will do this when they have listed as many, let us say, as seventeen. (234)

A genuinely loose or eccentric talker is a rare specimen to be prized.
(184)

The glistening tightness of the frog "grinning residually up," not to
mention its getting into the beer mug in the first place, is more reminiscent of British humorists like P. G. Wodehouse than of other British
philosophers. Felman believes that Austin's readers are quite wrong
not to consider the effect of the comedy turns he interjects throughout
his philosophical production. The man who saw as clearly as anyone
ever has that words do things was surely sensitive to the consequences
when one of the things they do is make us laugh.

The French psychoanalyst Jacques Lacan was famously adept at
integrating the most outrageous play with words into the most serious
work with them. Felman sees the fact that Lacan and Austin share an
irresistibly seductive ability to make us laugh and think at once as
resulting from ideas common to the thought both men convey. Despite
significant differences, psychoanalytic and speech-act theories engage
in a single enterprise, interrogation of the things humans do with
their symbolic representations of themselves. That is why Lacan and
Austin share "the same taste for paradox and the same self-subverting
consciousness of a breech at every point in knowledge" (Felman 1983;
p. 91). When he absorbed the constative into the performative, Felman's Austin joined Freud and his followers in attacking all positivist
conceptions of knowledge as grounded, firm and fixed.

In speech-act theory as in psychoanalysis, what we say we know is
not the result of observation but the process of fabrication. The two
fields are equally conscious that what matters in language is not
whether it's accurate but whether it's *felicitous*. If, like *fun, happy*
and its synonyms regularly crop up in the most solemn Austinian
expositions, it's because he shares the psychoanalytic insight that one
of the things we do with words is make a life we can get through. The
sexual sense of *performance* is therefore not without connection to
Austin's predilection for talking about it.

In terms of the problematic of the referent so often brought forward
in current philosophical and literary debates, Felman's Austin demonstrates with the same persistence as Freud and Lacan that the referent
comes from language rather than language from the referent.

> Neither for psychoanalysis nor for performative analysis is language
> a *statement* of the real, a simple reflection of the referent or its mimetic
> representation. Quite to the contrary, the referent is itself produced
> by language as its own *effect*. Both the analytic act and the performa-

tive are language effects—but referential language effects [. . .] The referent is no longer simply a preexisting *substance* but an *act*, that is, a dynamic movement of modification of reality. (76–77)

Felman sees speech-act theory's transcendence of the descriptive fallacy as simultaneously its institution of the truth of linguistic production. Austin and Lacan may be most alike in their visceral awareness that what language fails to do, describe a referent, is the foundational condition of possibility for every single one of the things it does.

According to the psychoanalytic model, we work out in our lives the structures organizing our psyches. Say those structures instill a need to be subordinate in romantic relationships (it sometimes happens). The person who feels subordinate will in all probability develop impeccably logical justifications for his or her inferiority: my partner's more intelligent, more successful, better looking, more important, more sensitive, etc. All those statements are fantasies, yet they all name reality as well because the subordinate person *lives out* the partner's superiority.

That's the sense in which the psychoanalytic referent is produced by language while also remaining real, and I find Felman's assimilation of the process to speech-act theory brilliant. Because the constative is also performative, it too produces what it names. Again we have referents—here all the facts society represents as true—that come from language but are lived out as well as invented by speakers. In Austin as surely as Lacan, what comes from language moves deeply through the rest of existence.

Felman applies the Lacanian Austin to an impressive range of topics. I am fully persuaded by her argument that inability to join in the fun is partly responsible for the "corrections" proposed by Jerrold Katz (1977) and Emile Benveniste (1971) that were discussed in Part One of this book, for example. Even when she fails to persuade, Felman always stimulates and provokes. Austin worked against as well as within the Anglo-American paradigms of analytic philosophy, and *The Literary Speech Act* is a constantly rewarding proof that he belongs in the tradition of continental philosophers with the greatest speculative scope.

As the subtitle *Don Juan with Austin* announces, Felman relates speech-act theory to a precise imaginary figure as well as an actual speculative current. She uses Austin's seductiveness to explain Don Juan's, especially as represented in Molière's *Don Juan*. No figure in the history of the human imagination has performed more spectacularly with language than Don Juan. He conquers women with words, promising them love, money, marriage, and whatever else they like in order to make them his. Felman argues that, since Don Juan never keeps any of the promises he makes, he also prefigures Austin by living out a deconstruction of the descriptive fallacy. His words work sensationally well, and they do so in total freedom from all referential constraints. Moreover, since Molière's Don Juan spends a vast amount of time explaining how he understands the words he uses, the play is a theoretical forerunner of *How to Do Things with Words* as well as a practical guide on how to do things with words.

Felman divides Molière's characters into two antagonistic camps separated by contrasted visions of language. Don Juan, who makes up one camp all by himself, conceives of words as not an expression of knowledge but a field of play, not a way to truth but a source of delight. The other camp includes all the remaining characters, unanimously convinced that language must state the case.

> What is really at stake in the play—the real conflict—is, in fact, the opposition between two views of language, one that is cognitive, or constative, and another that is performative. According to the cognitive view, which characterizes Don Juan's antagonists and victims, language is an instrument for transmitting *truth*, that is, an instrument of knowledge, a means of *knowing* reality. Truth is a relation of perfect congruence between an utterance and its referent, and, in a general way, between language and the reality it represents. (26–27)

Don Juan knows that language refers to itself alone. To make a promise, you say "I promise," and that's just what he says, over and over and over. Molière's drama thus agonistically confronts mutually exclusive concepts of language. One makes words refer, the other lets them thrill.

Felman's ingenious and original reading of Molière joins Fish's analysis of Shakespeare as a model application of Austin to practical criticism of classic theater. But even my schematic summary makes it clear that there are immense differences between the Austin Felman assimilates to Lacan and Freud and the Austin she applies to Molière. The first difference is that Austin's ultimate *integration* of the constative into the performative has been replaced by his original and discarded *opposition* between the two. The martial imagery Felman attaches to Molière's characters is also valid for their respective linguistic understandings. Constative and performative are here in overt hostilities even though Austin's repudiation of the contrast between them is crucial to speech-act theory's location among the deconstructive monuments of contemporary thought.

The second major difference between Felman's theoretical and practical invocations of Austin is the status of the extra-linguistic. As we saw, Felman insists that Austin's escape from the classic referent was, like Freud's, made possible by recognition that language creates—performs—a different sort of reality. But when the topic is Molière, reality and the referent are irredeemably delusionary. When Austin is with Lacan, the referent counts heavily; when he's with Don Juan, it doesn't count at all.

Compare the figure cut by the referent in the passages from *The Literary Speech Act* already quoted. "Both the analytic act and the performative are language effects—but referential language effects [. . .] The referent is no longer simply a preexisting *substance* but an *act*" (77). Rather than an italicized *act*, the referent is an hallucinated bogey when Felman considers Don Juan's antagonists and their constative conviction that "truth is a relation of perfect congruence between an utterance and its referent" (27). The constative that in theoretical exegesis gleefully dissects the descriptive fallacy is here its other name.

Does the constative produce or reproduce the referent? Felman answers in two ways. Considered with psychoanalysis, the Austinian category is productive; considered with Don Juan's enemies, reproductive. This striking variation may be a reluctance to accept Austin's conviction that language produces through its intersection with a community rather than, as in psychoanalysis, through its manipulation by an individual. The conventions making the constative perform aren't personal but social; the polis replaces the psyche. While Austin and psychoanalysis agree that the referent is an act, for Austin the act is collective.

No reader of this book needs reminding of the performative's dependence on social conventions. Let me just point out that the promise—the performative Don Juan exults in making absolutely anti-social—occasions Austin's most fervent pronouncement that performative speech and social adherence are one. "Accuracy and morality alike are on the side of the plain saying that *our word is our bond* [. . .] he *does* promise: the promise here is not even *void*, though it is given *in bad faith*" (Austin 1962; pp. 10–11). Promising, the speech act Felman sees as referring to nothing whatever except itself, is for Austin strong and direct reference to all those with whom we live and speak.

Felman gives the promise none of the referential value she elsewhere sees language enacting. "Don Juan is doing no more than playing on the self-referential property of these performative utterances [. . . He produces] the illusion of a real or extra-linguistic act of commitment created by an utterance that refers only to itself" (31). The assumption here is that commitment is real only if it's exclusively extra-linguistic. Yet speech-act theory's insight is that commitments are intra- and extra-linguistic at once, that the first thing we do with words is manifest intra-linguistically the extra-linguistic reality of the community whose conventions our words perform. As in Lacanian psychoanalysis, the referent of Austinian philosophy is in language; unlike psychoanalysis, Austin sees the referent permeating the world as well as the mind.

Felman's argument for capital points of intersection between Austin and influential contemporary theorists of signs-without-referents thus accompanies a less convincing argument that banishes the referent forever, that sternly contrasts constative and performative although Austin smoothly combined them. Somewhat paradoxically, *both* these components of Felman's *Literary Speech Act* help communicate the contribution speech-act theory makes to Western literary criticism at the end of the twentieth century. First, the ease with which Felman presents the traits common to Lacan and Austin—their mutual appreciation of language as play, their penchant for deconstructing logical oppositions, their simultaneous repudiation of the referent as pre-existent substance and validation of the referent produced by a semiotic act—makes it clear that speech-act theory is immune to standard objections to interpretations concerned with, to use Fish's terms once more, Reality, the Real World, Objective Facts. Like structuralism and post-structuralism, speech-act theory knows well that language is not a nomenclature, that verbal doing is vastly more interesting than verbal saying, that we will never understand words if we take their function to be reference to a world independent of them.

At the same time, speech-act theory incorporates the Real World of society as structuralism and post-structuralism have been unable to do. "Incorporates" is the wrong word; society and speech acts are mutually *constitutive*. Instead of being forever shut up in the prison house of language or the phantasms of the psyche, speech-act theory comes into being by recognizing the collective determinants of human existence and human speech. In order to put Austin on the side of the individual, Don Juan, and against society, all Molière's other characters, Felman must set aside both the social responsibility Austin attaches to the promise and the universal social connections that undo every opposition, especially war-like opposition, between constative and performative.

Like Searle, like Fish at certain moments, Felman signals deflection of Austin by interjection of God. Identifying the constative with the theological, she says that everyone in Molière's play except Don Juan reveres

> the word of God, in whose omniscience, indeed, language originates. Thus incarnating the authority of truth, God, or the "voice of Heaven" (that is, the fact that God speaks), underwrites the authority of language as a cognitive instrument. In this view, the sole function reserved for language is the *constative* function. (27)

When Austin definitively merges the constative into the performative, he definitively sets it in a human world where divinity is simply incongruous. Like all speech acts, the *constative* function is earthbound.

This is so even though the truth the constative speaks acquires through earthly processes all the solidity attributed to the divine logos. Like a bet or a marriage, a fact spoken felicitously is real within its social matrix. The constative is a subcategory of the performative because it too does *things* with words, because its effects too are referential language effects, no less referential for being in language. The constative power to produce truth is another essential distinction between Austinian and hegemonic literary theory. Felman calls Lacan and Austin "modern Don Juans" who *"know that truth is only an act"* (150). At least for Austin, that "only" is out of place; truth that is an act is by definition enacted as true. Language's freedom from facts brute and objective comes from its tight connection to facts institutional and social. In Austin's emphatic phrase, *our word is our bond* when we state a truth as when we make a promise. Facts collectively performed and lived are in situation every bit as powerful as the Word of God and the Voice of Heaven.

The Word of God appears to wield special power at the end of Molière's *Don Juan*, and Felman develops an impressive strategy for refuting the validation of the constative that God's might would seem to provide. Molière follows the myth by finally representing Don Juan consumed by fire, a flaming reminder that the Word retains and exercises its own arresting force. Felman, with astute concern for the ways classic texts can deconstruct themselves, points out that Don Juan's descent into hell does not conclude Molière's play. God appears and exits, the drama goes on. After divine punishment comes a celebrated comic scene in which Don Juan's servant Sganarelle bathetically mourns for the money Don Juan owes him. His master's eternal damnation means Sganarelle will be eternally unpaid, and the curtain falls on his tragicomic moan, "My wages, my wages, my wages!"

Felman contends that the end of *Don Juan* therefore does not show us that promises must be kept but reminds us that they are violated. Furthermore, divine punishment is what prevents Don Juan from meeting his payroll; instead of guaranteeing the sanctity of promises, eternal justice is actually the agent of their abrogation. If the text's purpose were to dramatize God's concern that humans keep their word, it could have ended on that concern in action. Since it in fact ends on the announcement that God leaves commitments forever unmet, the play dramatizes for Felman a commitment's irremediable separation from everything except the language articulating it. The last failure of God's word is God's failure to have the last word.

But Sganarelle has the stage to himself not only because God has disappeared; Don Juan is gone too. *Both* the figures whose antagonisms Felman reads as acting out the opposition between constative and performative are missing, but the play isn't over. It continues as Sganarelle's plea for language to count, for words to do things, for speech to act, for social reality to be real. If Don Juan's is the voice of the performative referring only to itself, if God's is the voice of the constative referring to absolute truth, then Sganarelle's is the voice that humanizes and conjoins what divine and mythic speakers keep separate. "My wages, my wages, my wages!" brings speech back to the human world, where the acts it performs are essential to survival. While God and Don Juan may well figure what Felman calls opposing views of language, Sganarelle figures exactly the reasons Austin brought the opposing views together.

So again we have a speech-act play, and again the reason is not the narrow characteristics of the play but the broad applicability of speech-act criticism, especially to the drama. They were chosen for other reasons, but the plays discussed in this chapter represent what may be the three most fertile social environments for theatrical creation the West has known since antiquity. Louis XIV's France (*Don Juan*), Golden Age Spain (*Estrella of Seville, Secret Vengeance for Secret Insult*), and Elizabethan England (*Edward II, Coriolanus*) gave us an astounding number of the plays we have enshrined as masterpieces, and those masterpieces have in turn inspired highly influential demonstrations of Austinian contributions to theatrical interpretation. Nothing more clearly shows the reasons speech-act theory and drama are both coterminous with *performance* than the prominence of classic theater in the classic essays of speech-act criticism.

To extend Richard Ohmann's metaphor, it's not just a play's action that rides on the train of illocutions. Illocutions *are* the play, in its entirety. What they constitute is an integral whole that simultaneously comes from and gives rise to each illocution taken individually.

This cause-and-effect, effect-and-cause dialectic in theater furnishes a singularly expressive analogy for the reciprocal relationship of society and language in Austinian philosophy. As Fish pointed out in the memorable phrase that concludes his study of Coriolanus's determination to greet no more, a very great deal rides on the "agreement (forever being renewed) to say 'Good Morrow' " (Fish 1980; p. 245).

7

The Prose of the World

Austinian criticism of other genres has been neither so fully developed nor so widely discussed as the theater's speech-act core. Several of the discussions of poetry listed in my bibliography are admittedly first steps toward an analytic paradigm, and some introduce a higher degree of technical sophistication than is appropriate here. Despite individual differences among them, however, all interesting speech-act analyses of poetry rely on the same insight into language's collective matrix that animates criticism of theater. Because the devices traditionally enshrined as poetic are always already social as well, no student of poetry should ignore the conventions that make them work even when part of the work they do is remove themselves from the conventions applying elsewhere. "Metaphoring is itself a speech act very much like stating or commanding" (Mack 1975; p. 247); we can no more see metaphor as autonomous because it cuts itself off from a referent than we can see a command as magic because it moves an army. In both cases, the force is conventionally not internally generated.

C. Carroll Hollis (1983) has studied the specifically poetic effect of illocutionary action in Walt Whitman's *Leaves of Grass*. Hollis emphasizes Whitman's predilection for explicitly performative verbs in their classic first-person, present-indicative, declarative-active form. Lines that do what they say—"I bequeath myself," "I give myself," "I speak the password primeval"—proliferate through all versions of *Leaves of Grass*. Their effect is uniformly to emphasize the message implicitly conveyed whenever a performative takes: speaker and audience share a world and have a common engagement with the conventions that keep their world whole. For Hollis, Whitman's power is integrally bound up with the fact that "he went over and over his lines, asserting, then clarifying and emphasizing, their illocutionary force" (Hollis 1983; p. 123).

In Whitman as elsewhere, the point is much broader than the textual prominence of a certain kind of verb. Quantity becomes quality, illocutionary language performs the illocutionary universe of mutual dependence and reciprocal impact. The physical intimacy of a Whitmanesque line like "lift me close to your face till I whisper" interacts with the social intimacy of common validation of collective identity. The conventions of Rule A.1 require that speakers be committed to them if words are to do something, and Whitman's performative lines constantly plead for collaboration in keeping this commitment strong. Sequences like "I celebrate myself/And what I assume you shall assume" make explicit the connection between overt performative (I celebrate myself) and shared conventions (we shall assume together); the connection holds for the many other performative verbs in *Leaves of Grass*. Because speech acts and speakers interact at once, Whitman's remarkable illocutionary lexicon *effects* the same democratic spirit he obsessively extols.

With prose fiction, speech-act criticism has concentrated on dialogue. The special vocation of theatrical techniques for revealing that saying and doing are one holds even when those techniques appear in other genres. Fiction too uses affirmation or denial of dialogic success to convey the solidity or fragility of connections among speakers. Between book covers as between rising and falling curtains, the dialectic between illocutionary felicity and collective life is a major literary theme.

When critics apply Austin's categories to the speech acts represented in prose, they commonly ignore the attacks on representation often made by contemporary literary theory. We must suspend our doubts concerning the validity of representation and mimesis when we directly apply the speech-act vision of words in the world to literary arrangements of words in fiction. This suspension can pay off handsomely. The stakes of felicitous verbal performance are as high in fiction as outside it, and Austinian analysis contributes markedly to explaining why. Speech-act criticism of prose has joined theatrical analysis in concentrating on the ways overtly performative verbs express an illocutionary community.

Emphasis on the overt performative has the effect of obscuring Austin's definition of constative language as a covert performative, however. It establishes a hierarchy that can impede exploitation of Austin's potential contribution to *resolving* the problem of mimesis. The strong objections to mimetic readings among recent literary theorists have understood representational literature as a variant of the descriptive fallacy. A mimetically oriented reader seeing nineteenth-century London in Dickens or nineteenth-century Paris in Balzac is supposedly guilty of sweeping words aside to find what's beyond them, and it makes precious little sense for a student of literature to think words don't matter. They are after all what literature is.

Assaults on mimesis proceed logically from literary theorists' dismissal of Referent, Reality, Real World, Objective Facts. Turning our attention to language and turning our back on the referent are the same motion, and it effects a double refusal of mimesis. Illegitimate for supposing that the referent matters, mimetic interpretation is also unserviceable by virtue of its failure to set language first. The linguistic turn in criticism has meant the death and early sorrow of all literary concepts that, like mimesis, entail extra-linguistic preoccupations.

As Felman showed, Austin's own upsurges against the descriptive fallacy place him among philosophers and critics who attend constantly to language. Yet his own linguistic focus is never exclusive. Because speech-act theory thoroughly compounds the linguistic and extra-linguistic, the referent can't be dismissed out of hand. To introduce an assessment to which we'll return, Jacques Derrida says this about Austin's contribution to the philosophy of language: "the performative does not have its referent (but here that word is certainly no longer appropriate, and this precisely is the interest of the discovery) outside of itself or, in any event, before and in front of itself" (Derrida 1988a; p. 13). So adept is Austin's unification of language and its other that the referent is always both there and not there, which is why Derrida must both say "referent" and classify what he says as "certainly" inappropriate. The continental masters of doubt among whom Felman and others persuasively set Austin ground their insights on the referent's eternal absence; Austin's theory is concomitant with the referent's presence in all the things we do with words.

As a subcategory of the performative, the constative also has reality within itself. For the constative too, we must both say "referent" and apologize for it. It's this duality that offers a potential resolution of the vexed problem of mimesis. From an Austinian viewpoint, nineteenth-century London and nineteenth-century Paris are not some reified substance, out there, in and of themselves, before or in front or outside representation. They are the performance, forever in process, of those who inhabit them, the collectivity whose interlocking verbal and nonverbal relationships simultaneously constitute and represent a social formation. The people for whom London and Paris were a habitat did exactly the same thing as Dickens, Balzac, and the other authors for whom those cities were a setting: perform a reality in the process of stating one. Speech-act criticism repels every principled objection to literary mimesis on the ground that mimetic understanding requires connecting incommensurable entities; the unification of language and its referent is accomplished every time speech acts, and speech acts all the time.

Paul Ricoeur has suggested that we reorient the debate over mimesis by recognizing the mimetic character of our existence as well as our fictions. Representation, far from restricted to literature, is essential to everyday life, and Ricoeur "playfully yet seriously" (1981b; p. 17) introduces subscripts—mimesis$_1$, mimesis$_2$—to mark the simultaneous identity and distinctions among human performances of reality and representation of performances. Mimesis$_1$ is what we do outside literature, mimesis$_2$ what we do within it, and the numerical variation must be understood in conjunction with the verbal constant. Like Austin's referent, Ricoeur's mimesis is simultaneously enclosed in language and loose in the world.

The genre of prose fiction that has occasioned the most heated discussion of the referent's status in mimetic literature is sociohistorical realism, especially as found in Balzac, Stendhal, and their successors among French novelists. In *Realism and Revolution*, I developed an Austinian approach to the "realist constative" as simultaneously a literary and a historical performance of social reality. French realism arose during the Bourbon Restoration, the period when a monarchist regime represented itself as ruling by divine right even though decades of revolutionary upheaval had clearly shown that, as Marlowe knew, kingship is not a gift from God but the conventional effect of conventional procedures. "Ruling by divine right" became a felicitous utterance despite the many referential circumstances that denounced it as false and grotesque; while it was doing so, Balzac and Stendhal were inventing literary techniques that would also show the world why fact and fiction cannot be reliably divided off. Social and stylistic enactment of the referent, mimesis$_1$ and mimesis$_2$, were in striking coincidence while the West's exemplary representational form came into being.

When contemporary literary critics have addressed realist prose, they have emphasized the cogent reasons we cannot consider it referential in the non-Austinian sense. All language, including its realist version, refuses to be a nomenclature, for the things words say can never give direct access to things unsaid. If we give the referent its Austinian sense, however, then realism's refusal simply to name hasn't the slightest pertinence to its historical representations. Within the realist constative, social and verbal configurations enact rather than repel one another. If a fictional society presents multiple points of contact with historical analogues, it's because historical societies also rely on realist techniques. Realism and Austinian philosophy both know that the constative can also be felicitous, that words can produce reality when they say things as well as when they do them.

That's why the attitudes toward realism and Austinian philosophy among prominent literary theorists present many striking parallels. In both cases, an immense amount has been written about the referent denied; in neither case has the referent performed attained comparable visibility. When mentioned at all, Austin's dramatic insertion of constative language into the performative schema has usually appeared as yet another logical opposition collapsing under the shock of linguistic detonations; seldom have the facts produced through constative performance, the monument erected when the terrain is razed, been accorded attention.

Contemporary revelation of realism's verbal play has left its social content analogously underexplored and unloved. The hugely influential analysis of Balzac in Roland Barthes's *S/Z*, for instance, argues that realist devotion to historical precision makes you want to throw up whenever you run into it on the page; language with social connections is a dead weight preventing literature from becoming itself. Realist prose can for Barthes make you quiver with pleasure as well, but only when it stops trying to be realistic. Realism and speech-act theory share a sociohistorical core that current literary theory has neglected for the linguistic delight they also both provide.

With realism as with speech-act theory, however, validation of the sociohistorical in no way requires solemnizing and regimenting the linguistic. To the contrary: language's liberation from the brute facts of objective reality is the *precondition* for its ability to perform the lived truths of collective existence. Realism's verbal arabesques and pirouettes, which contemporary critics have taken to cut it off from history, are in fact what makes history accessible to it. The performative force of constative language is inoperative in words that submit themselves to descriptive (rather than productive) duties. Realism's many internal refutations of the assumption that it's just describing external reality are essential to its illustration of the speech-act axiom that reality is external and internal to language at once.

Written in 1830, Stendhal's *The Red and the Black* is close to the earliest novel now universally admitted into the realist canon. Historians have long joined with literary critics in praising its stunning representation of the private and public realities characteristic of Restoration France. The beginning of this beginning encapsulates realism's constitutive mix of verbal play and historical work, the same mix allowing Austin to repudiate the descriptive fallacy while (and by) emphasizing language's social identity. Stendhal's subtitle is variously "Chronicle of 1830" and "Chronicle of the XIXth Century," either of which puts the text that follows among the works of history that set language to unrelievedly referential tasks. Yet that subtitle appears with a title that, by declining to refer, gives the same text a wholly different generic specification. Critical explanations of what "red" and "black" denote are multifarious and incompatible; considered together, they coalesce in a demonstration that the title's function is not to denote anything whatever. Depending on the reader, "red" and "black" refer to the army and the church, revolution and reaction, the spaces on a roulette wheel or simply the fashionability of color terms in novel titles while Stendhal was writing. The "chronicle" starts with a pair of terms suggesting that language cannot accomplish a chronicle's representational tasks at all.

The mix gets murkier. An "editor" announces that there's reason to believe the novel was written in 1827, which means that the chronicle of 1830 is the phantasmatic invention of 1830. The novel's epigraph, "The truth, the bitter truth. *Danton*," would go back to history and those who make it except that Danton never said "The truth, the bitter truth"; even the real figures of the real world come attached to language that makes their reality questionable, as the epigraph to the first chapter also shows.

> Put thousands together,
> Less bad
> But the cage less gay.
> Hobbes

Hobbes of course never said any such thing, nor did anyone else for whom language is supposed to make sense. The inherent incomprehensibility of what "Hobbes" said is contextually magnified by the fact that this epigraph appears in English rather than in the French of the novel it begins. The opening words of *The Red and the Black* teasingly deny each of their own suggestions that a novel can or should represent history.

But the hundreds of pages following the introductory words became and remain a textbook display that the novel can and does represent history. Stendhal's playful insurrections against the possibility of realist literature are the prolegomenon for his monumental contribution to creating it. Like Austin, Stendhal begins with verbal performance and proceeds to constative representation; as with Austin, his beginning doesn't contradict but enables his conclusion. The Austinian and realist constative are no less dependent on language's refusal to name than on its ability to state.

I want here to continue the discussion of the realist constative begun in *Realism and Revolution* by examining a Balzac novella called *Adieu*. Like *The Red and the Black*, *Adieu*, also written in 1830, is one of the works in which the realist project was first worked out. It too comments powerfully on the nature of the constative language it's in the process of creating.

Adieu is divided into three parts, the first of which introduces the protagonists and presents the mystery of their relationship. While hunting with a friend, Philippe de Sucy, a former officer in Napoleon's army, comes upon a secluded property where he sees a woman with all the appearances of raving insanity. Her hair and clothes are a mess, she jumps in and out of trees like a squirrel, she rolls in the grass like a colt, and her only use of human speech is to repeat the word "Adieu" in a voice that reveals neither thought nor feeling. When she pushes her hair away from her face, however, Philippe falls in a dead faint, for he has recognized the disheveled maniac as the countess Stéphanie de Vandières, the only woman he's ever loved.

Philippe and Stéphanie had last seen each other seven years before when, during the Napoleonic army's retreat from Moscow in 1812, Philippe was captured after helping Stéphanie and her wounded husband to escape from the horrors of the French rout by the Russians at the Berezina river. The second part of *Adieu* is a flashback that describes the ghastly events at the Berezina in vivid detail. This retrospective narrative concludes with Stéphanie floating away from Philippe on an overcrowded raft in the ice-choked river. Stéphanie's husband falls into the water and dies, but she can do nothing except shout a final "Adieu" as Philippe collapses on the riverbank from cold, regret, and fatigue.

Balzac's third part returns to the present and describes Philippe's determination to cure Stéphanie's insanity and live happily ever after with her. He's undaunted when he learns that Stéphanie, her mind destroyed by the 1812 retreat, has spent the intervening seven years in so pathological a condition that she made herself sexually available to uncounted men of every class and even refused for a period to wear clothes altogether. Philippe is certain that, despite everything, he can triumph over the past and bring his beloved back to her senses. He holds her in the old way, speaks to her of their old love, cares for her with the old tenderness, but her only response is an occasional "Adieu," still spoken in a voice expressing neither thought nor feeling, without "her soul communicating a single discernible inflection to this word" (Balzac; p. 200. All translations from *Adieu* are my own).

At last, on the verge of suicidal despair, Philippe takes a desperate step. He leaves Stéphanie and constructs the setting for an elaborate psychodrama by converting a section of his property into a life-sized replica of the fatal countryside around the Berezina. A Griffith or von Stroheim *avant la lettre*, Philippe also enrolls vast numbers of people to fill his stage and takes attentive care that he and his supporting cast look exactly right. When all the preparations needed to reproduce the past are complete, Philippe brings in Stéphanie to relive the night she lost her mind. The hope is of course that what drove sanity away can restore it, but the plan is only partially successful. The light of reason does return to Stéphanie's eyes, she recognizes Philippe and says that she loves him, but she also utters a final "Adieu" and falls dead. After a brief and heroic attempt to forget, Philippe joins his lover in death by blowing his brains out.

Adieu was known to few people other than Balzac specialists before 1974, when it appeared in a paperback edition edited by Patrick Berthier with an introduction by Pierre Gascar. Gascar's introduction, a fine example of the mimetic reading that used to dominate critical approaches to realist prose, highlights the "most gripping realism" (Gascar 1974; p. 17. Translations from Gascar are my own) characterizing *Adieu*'s representation of war. For Gascar, this story is among the very first texts in world literature to give verbal expression to the brutal truth of martial life. Balzac decisively broke with dominant literary conventions of military glory and produced something radically new. Thanks to the "realism, without precedent in the history of literature, with which war is here presented" (9), Balzac's battle scenes "suffice to give war its real face: that is, its contemporary face [. . .] Balzac inaugurates the modern form of horror" (12).

For Gascar, this text's achievement is therefore supremely referential. Balzac gives war its real face and sets the reader in front of it. Old literary forms were inadequate to the horror of the total war that became real with Napoleon and his armies, and Balzac consequently changed literary form in response to the changed face of reality. Gascar's underlying assumptions, mimetic and referential, are that literature always *can* describe faithfully and responsibly and that the best literature, that deserving to be called realistic, invariably *does*. In the place of lying words imposed by a corrupt literary tradition, *Adieu* introduces language capable of effacing itself before the truth of its object.

The year after Gascar and Berthier's edition, Shoshana Felman put their reading through the wringer in an essay entitled "Women and Madness: The Critical Phallacy," which applies the categories and concerns of high deconstruction to the text where Gascar found the truth of history. Felman points out that Gascar's reading depends on ignoring two of the three parts of *Adieu*, those dealing with a woman and her madness, in order to focus solely on the middle section, which deals with men and their manly occupations. For Felman, it's not by accident that this act of repression is performed in the name of realism: the real and the manly are ideological constructs with reciprocally invigorating powers. "What, then, is this 'realism' the critic here ascribes to Balzac, if not the assumption, not shared by the text, that what happens to men is more important, and/or more 'real,' than what happens to women?" (Felman 1975; p. 6). Gascar negates the woman and validates the real because his emphasis and his neglect both help naturalize the male/female hierarchy.

Felman argues that to see here the great literary discovery of how to represent the reality of war is perverse: it ignores the text's lesson on the death blow feminine difference strikes against every reliable representation of the real. In the long futility of Philippe's desperate efforts to make Stéphanie stop saying "Adieu" and speak his name, the text configures the absurdity of every attempt dependably to attach words and referents. Philippe keeps begging Stéphanie to say who he is, Stéphanie keeps saying "Adieu, adieu, adieu," and Felman reads this cataclysmic breakdown of the communicative circuit as eradicating all the tools realism needs.

> To [Philippe's] demand for recognition and for the restoration of identity through language, through the authority of proper names, Stéphanie opposes, in the figure of her madness, the dislocation of any transitive, communicative language, of "propriety" as such, of any correspondence or transparency joining "names" to "things," the blind opacity of a lost signifier unmatched by any signified, the pure recurrent difference of a word detached from both its meaning and its context. (9)

In the woman's refusal to name the man begging for recognition, Felman sees language's irremediable dissipation of the power on which realism depends absolutely. We confront here the hopeless impossibility of "*any* correspondence or transparency joining 'names' to 'things.'"

In their mutually exclusive concepts and values, Felman and Gascar's essays typify the impasse over realist mimesis. In the same seventy-page tale, the deconstructionist sees the "madness of the signifier" (10), the historical critic sees the signifier finally coming to its senses and saying what war actually is. The deconstructionist sees the unmanageable metonymies of language's nightmarish "*lack of resemblance*" (8) to its referents, the historical critic sees language with so perfect a resemblance to its referent that the reader lives all the horrors let slip by the dogs of war.

This combination—a founding realist text that recounts a thoroughly historicized narrative, a classically mimetic reading that understands the text as a faithful description of reality, an exemplarily deconstructive reading that denies both this text and any other the power of descriptive relation to reality—encapsulates issues that have sparked some of the most absorbing debates in recent literary theory. I want to argue here that a speech-act criticism can productively intervene in those debates by reformulating the issues. It's obviously also of interest that Felman does for Balzac precisely what she does for Austin: develop a brilliant, even breathtaking interpretation of linguistic fireworks without addressing the socialized ground the rockets shoot up from. Once more, the vision shared by realism and speech-act theory is perhaps clearest in the similar responses they elicit from contemporary critics.

The first speech-act reformulation of the issues raised by *Adieu* is that, with the descriptive fallacy eliminated, the question of whether the text's words do or don't "resemble" their referent just can't come up. When we *do* things with words, the referent is neither captured nor alienated; it's produced through a process that contradicts both the historicist assumption that written description is perfect and the deconstructionist conviction that writing is supra-historical. The Austinian concept of socialized verbal performance unites Gascar's orientation toward historical specificity with Felman's orientation toward language that by its nature cannot specify.

If we substitute the constative for the referential, the justification for Gascar's praise becomes not *Adieu*'s descriptive success but rather the intertextual rebellion in Balzac's representation of war. What matters is less the adequacy of Balzac's language to the army led by Napoleon than its refusal of the armies written by other authors. The felicity of constative representation comes from the conventions observed by a collectivity, and Balzac weakened dominant conventions in a language event that matters regardless of whether it conforms dependably to events outside language.

I argued in Part One that Austin's implicit "I state" and "we assert" are crucial because people perform communal solidarity when they *say* the same thing with words as effectively as when they use words to *do* the same thing. The logical consequence is that different constatives undo communal solidarity as much as contradictory declarations or incompatible marriage rites. For a speech-act criticism, that Balzac wrote war in a new way counts much more than whether he described it accurately. His unprecedented representation meant that received conventional procedures were no longer having their conventional effect.

Gascar is actually quite sensitive to the distance between war in *Adieu* and in other fictions, and we can share his admiration for Balzac's distance from his predecessors without agreeing that the distance is due to a perfect congruence of Balzacian language and objective reality. Even the most evangelical anti-representationalists find some representations—of war, of gender, of race, of class—more objectionable than others, and Balzac's stylistic novelties are a step away from the wrong direction despite the theoretical objections to calling them a step in the right direction. To make horror, in Gascar's words the modern form of horror, integral to the experience of reading about soldiery is a literary achievement of no small historical substance.

If the constative can reformulate Gascar's historicist point so as to make it more compatible with recent literary theory, can it put Felman's deconstructive moves in touch with history? I want to develop an affirmative answer by looking at the section of *Adieu* that, as Felman has every reason to insist, presents remarkable resemblances to the realist project as a whole: Philippe's reconstruction of the Berezina plain as it was the night Stéphanie lost her mind. When Philippe sets out to bring Russia into his backyard, he makes laughably evident the impossibility of representation actually incorporating an objective referent. When, as the text puts it he "achieve[s] his goal" (210), his success urges us to contemplate the difference between successful representation and incorporating an objective referent. Philippe *performs* a truth that has nothing to do with objective reality but everything to do with the conventional procedures of constative communities.

The parallels between the way *Adieu* describes Philippe's undertaking and the way traditional criticism describes realist fiction in general are remarkable. Philippe too "succeeded in copying" (209) the past in the present, he too created an all-encompassing representation of what actually was. "He ordered uniforms and faded clothing in order to costume several hundred peasants. He built huts, bivouacs and fortifications and burned them out. In the end he forgot nothing of what could reproduce the most horrible of all scenes, and he achieved his goal" (210). Pierre Gascar's appreciation of what Balzac did in Part Two of *Adieu* is almost interchangeable with *Adieu*'s appreciation of what Philippe did in Part Three.

Felman therefore understands Philippe's realist authorship the same way as Gascar's realist criticism. She reads the double death concluding *Adieu* as announcing that representation is always fatal to the humans and texts accepting it. "Through this paradoxical and disconcerting ending, the text subverts and dislocates the logic of representation which it has dramatized through Philippe's endeavor and his failure. Literature thus breaks away from pure representation; when transparency and meaning, 'reason' and 'representation' are regained, when madness ends, so does the text itself" (Felman 1975; pp. 9–10). In other terms, history *can* be represented, for Philippe does succeed in bringing 1812 back to life in 1820. But this success of historical representation kills the woman, her madness, and literature. From Felman's perspective, the text destroys itself when its characters relive a precise moment from the past because every representation of the past is inimical to textuality.

To concentrate on "Philippe's endeavor and his *failure*," however, skirts the fact that the endeavor at first succeeds. Philippe's representation of the past is a textual presence before it "subverts and dislocates" the text. It makes Stéphanie sane again, and the association of her madness with textuality gives this therapeutic success implications no less far-reaching than the ultimately fatal outcome. Part Three of *Adieu* is entitled "The Cure," and the word is not merely ironic. Balzac's prose is lyrically specific about representation's vivifying effects. When she enters Philippe's artificial world, Stéphanie sees, feels, and speaks once again. The language describing her rebirth, unrestrained and exuberant, joins italics and exclamation points to an insistently vitalistic lexicon.

> She jerked her head toward Philippe and *saw him* [. . .] Color feebly began to return to Stéphanie's beautiful face; then, finally, shade by shade, she recovered all the radiance of a young girl's gleaming freshness [. . .] Life and happiness, animated by a burning intelligence, passed from part to part like a fire [. . .] Stéphanie's eyes threw out a celestial ray, a vivid flame. She was living, she was thinking! [. . .] God Himself untied that dead tongue a second time and once more cast His fire into that extinguished soul. Human will came with its electric rush and vivified this body from which it had so long been absent. (213–214)

The fire and light imagery is remarkable, as is its attribution to God Himself. This passage could describe the Sistine Chapel ceiling except that God here conveys the spark of life to Eve instead of Adam.

When life culminates in speech, Stéphanie finally names Philippe and then, just before she dies, gives back meaning to what she elsewhere makes a gapingly empty signifier, the word "Adieu." "Oh, it's Philippe [. . .] Adieu, Philippe. I love you, adieu!" (214). Before it kills her, representation gives Stéphanie the warmth of life, the power of reason, and the control of language.

Let's defer the quandary of how this literal apotheosis of realism—

its textual conversion into the God of Genesis making what it represents live, breathe, and move—can without transition develop into textual definition of realist representation as a death-dealing poison. For the present, I want to consider another riveting contrast, that between Philippe's power over Stéphanie here and his earlier helplessness before her. The page that describes Stéphanie's metamorphosis is stunning even in isolation. It becomes dumbfounding in the context of page after page that earlier presented the agent of her metamorphosis as comically ineffectual.

Moreover, the contrast between the man's success and failure in reaching the woman coincides exactly with the presence and absence of representation. As a character in a tableau, Philippe is omnipotent; as himself, he is abject. When he *represents* a lover, Philippe controls Stéphanie's vision, soul, voice, and mind. When he *is* a lover, he's wretchedly unable to elicit the slightest response. The distinction is between the referential and the constative, between reality in itself and reality as performed; in *Adieu* the referential is a bad joke, the constative a great power.

It's after the repeatedly experienced futility of contact with Stéphanie in his own person that Philippe decks himself out as the person he no longer is. The woman to whom "life and happiness" return when she sees a disguised Philippe in an artificial landscape displays only stupor and unconcern when she sees and touches the real Philippe in a natural landscape. The text goes daringly far in specifying the titillating character of the touching that doesn't work.

> She soon grew accustomed to sitting down on him, to wrapping her lean, agile arm around him. In this position, so dear to lovers, Philippe would slowly give sweets to the avid countess [. . .] she let him run his hands through her hair, allowed him to take her in his arms, and received burning kisses without pleasure. (204)

To Philippe's ardor, Stéphanie responds with chilling indifference; to his stage set, her response involves every fiber of her being. If Philippe's reproduction of Russia in France figures realism's reproduction of the world in a book, then the demonstration in *Adieu* that realism works follows a prior demonstration that reality fails miserably. When Philippe takes Stéphanie on his lap and tells her what he feels and who he is, when referent and representation are in seamless conjunction, nothing happens. When Philippe brings Stéphanie to the space he has artistically transformed into an illusion, when referent and representation are a continent and a decade apart, everything happens. In this very early working-out of the literary forms that would impose the Balzacian model, the power of realism stands in point by point opposition to the impotence of reality.

Yet realism is also in point by point *association* with the conventional procedures that identify the speech act. When the referential goes out, the constative comes in. Philippe "succeeded in copying the riverbank in his park" (209) by adjusting his representational undertaking to a multilateral vision of what the riverbank was, that shared by himself and those who were with him, including, he hopes, Stéphanie. This is the sense in which the constative is historical without being referential; it adjusts itself not to what is but to what is thought. The tonic shock of recognition comes from a stage set's conformity to the mental image Philippe holds in common with others: "he recognized the Berezina. This false Russia was of so frightful a truth that several of his companions in arms recognized the scene of their old sufferings" (210).

Louis Althusser and other theorists of ideology have insisted on the gap between authentic cognition and the deluded re-cognition that constitutes a society's mythic understanding of itself. That gap is apparent here, in the double occurrence of the word "recognized" to designate Philippe and his comrades' vivid apperception of what they cannot perceive because it isn't there. Like Althusser, however, Balzac's text is far from dismissing false recognition as inconsequential. It performs a world as well as concealing one.

In a deconstructive reading, the text would have to be deriding and undoing itself when it sets "recognized" in a context where recognition is objectively impossible. In a speech-act reading, the point is rather that objective facts aren't pertinent to constative felicity: we find reality where we put it. Look again at the language *Adieu* invokes to articulate its characters' perception of a presence in an absence. A "frightful truth" adheres to Philippe's "false Russia," as later an "awful truth" (211) will emerge from his false appearance. This commingling of truth and falsity is the crucial feature in constative expression of the truth society validates regardless of falsity. Realism addresses what a collectivity accepts as real, and this early realist narrative makes that generic feature its lesson as well as its armature.

Realist depiction of the constative consequently does not contest but confirms the sign's untethering from all determinant origins, from every objective ground. Again, the collaboration between semiosis and ideology, realism's subject of choice, would be impossible were signs in fact a nomenclature: language can perform what's lived in society solely because it doesn't name what is in reality. Philippe's discovery that performance is required because reality isn't performing will be repeated throughout the realist canon.

The specific achievement of Philippe's representation is to restore Stéphanie's womanhood as constatively depicted, which is to say as ideologically and socially constructed. It's hard to think of an early nineteenth-century text as concerned as *Adieu* with the distinction between gender, a constative social construct, and sex, a referential cluster of physiological features. Philippe can take possession of the insane Stéphanie's physiology by feeding her sweets, but he experiences only burning despair when he does so. He even defines womanhood as precisely what's lacking in the body on his lap. Because he knew Stéphanie "when," as he puts it, "she was a woman" (202), he finds nothing womanly in the hair between his fingers or the lips he covers with burning kisses while taking the "position so dear to lovers."

Social determination of Philippe's understanding of femininity is also apparent in the gestures that accompany his constative representation of the Berezina plain. Throughout "The Cure," he is active, Stéphanie passive. As with Pygmalion, the man gives life, the woman accepts it; the man is the artist, the woman the work. The hierarchy is clear, and it comes as no surprise that Stéphanie's return to life is also her recovery of what social discourse says a woman ought to have, a beautiful face that glows for her lover with "all the radiance of a young girl's gleaming freshness." Moreover, she presumably dies because her seven years of nakedness and sexual license have made her what social discourse says a woman cannot be. When that discourse regains its sway, Stéphanie suffocates under the crushing weight constative womanhood brings with it. Reentry into representation fails to provide a life worth living.

Yet *Adieu* strongly argues that there's no life worth living outside of representation either. Within historical time, social constructs are the only sort we've got. That which kills Stéphanie is the same thing that brings her back to life. Besides "feminine" attributes like a glowing complexion and a loving voice, she also regains "happiness and life," "human will," "burning intelligence." Stéphanie's passage from life to death is so sudden that the text invents a new word—*elle se cadavérisa*, she corpsified herself (214)—to specify it. Her passage from death to life is equally dramatic, and the same agency is responsible for both transformations. What representation takes away is no more than what it has just given.

During the time the insane Stéphanie was not a woman, neither was she a human being. Her maniacal "Adieu" refuses human existence as well as repudiating orderly semiosis, and Felman is careful not to suggest that the pure iteration of a lost signifier gives Stéphanie the identity she eradicates in others. "Woman and Madness: The Critical Phallacy" approvingly quotes Phyllis Chesler's denial of every "intention to romanticize madness, or to confuse it with political or cultural revolution" (Felman 1975; p. 2). Although death is within social discourse, outside it is nothingness.

The consequence seems clear, and again speech-act theory and realism agree on it. In order to produce a bearable existence, in order to make the political or cultural revolution that insanity is not, constative discourse must be changed. Repudiating it is not enough. There's still no world elsewhere. To remain in a society is to live its constative representations as well as its performative conventions; to transform conventions and representations is to transform society. Language bears within it all the things it does.

It's probable that part of Balzac's inspiration for *Adieu* was the story of Victor, the Wild Child of Aveyron, a wolf boy whom Jean Itard tried to bring into language with dogged but ultimately futile dedication. Itard's descriptions of his experience with Victor were widely read and discussed in their day, and they remain absorbing and thought-provoking, so much so that they inspired an excellent movie by François Truffaut (*L'Enfant sauvage* [1970]). The theme of Itard's narratives about Victor is that language isn't a contingent adjunct to the human condition but an essential constituent of it, and that theme remains prominent in Balzac's novella. Like Victor the wolf boy, Stéphanie is outside language and the things it does because she's beyond human beings and the ways they live; like him, she must acquire social and verbal reality at once.

Socioverbal reality is inevitably historicized, and *Adieu* scrupulously provides the historical coordinates of the representation it simultaneously denounces and reenacts. Stéphanie comes back to life in the France of 1820, where her sexual adventures are exactly what they were when she passed out seven years before, an activity that cannot be tolerated in one sex however understandable it may be in the other. As a drafter of the Napoleonic Code put it, "the wife's unfaithfulness implies more corruption and has more dangerous effects than the husband's." Stéphanie dies for the same reason France's civil code punished female infidelity by prison and male infidelity by a fine, because social discourse was incapable of incorporating women except through the forms required by men.

Despite its shocking representational inadequacy, however, social discourse had the whole force of a repressive state apparatus behind it. There are excellent historical reasons why Balzac's working title for *Adieu* was *A Woman's Duty*. The famous Article 213 of the Napoleonic Code reads "The wife owes obedience to her husband"; exactly like the legislative pronouncement that a woman's unfaithfulness has more dangerous effects than a man's, that article pretends to describe without prescribing, wants to be merely constative without performing. But the constative is always also performative, and this seeming statement was actually in hyperactive collaboration with all the prescriptive language through which Stéphanie's society policed and controlled its members.

Article 213, which became a fearsome existential truth in blithe unconcern for its conventional fabrication, is directly comparable to more recent legislative efforts to combine the supposedly referential proposition that human life begins at conception with the performative apparatus needed to make that lie oppressively truthful as well. The real in realism is exactly this kind of speech act, the fabrication of lived reality from phantasmatic verbal inventiveness. Philippe's failure to get through when he's a man and his total communicative success when he's a realist character manifest the capital insight shared by realism and speech-act theory: language's expressive force always reveals not the nature of the world but the will of a collectivity. Because constative representation works through the pressure exerted by those who accept it, denouncing its illusions while ignoring the forces mustered behind them misses the point.

To help make the point, Parts One and Three of *Adieu* situate Stéphanie's annihilated subjectivity in the Bourbon Restoration as firmly as Part Two ascribes the origin of her madness to the Napoleonic adventure. Considered in relation to social conventions, this insistence on the stasis of a madwoman's condition across radical transformations of her nation is highly suggestive. Stéphanie insanely says the same word over and over while her countrymen are changing their government again and again. Between Stéphanie's first and last utterances of her meaningless "Adieu," France went from the Emperor to a king, came back to the Emperor, then brought back the king and gave him a free hand to extirpate all memory of the Empire and its acts.

Among the acts the king chose not to extirpate was the Empire's violent relegation of woman to the endless status of man's ward. Whatever vestiges of female autonomy France possessed were eliminated when the Napoleonic Code gave husbands the same authority over their wives that fathers possessed over their underaged daughters. There are sound historical grounds for female language's maniacal upsurge against the male desire for verbal recognition during the early post-Napoleonic era. Stéphanie refuses to give Philippe the same thing society refuses to give her. The seven years in which she mindlessly repeated the same detached signifier coincide with seven years in which almost nothing in French life stayed the same except for the legal, cultural, and political incrustation of woman's place on women's lives.

Because constative representation performs manliness as well as femininity, there are tighter connections among the three parts of *Adieu* than might at first appear. One of the intertexts contested by Balzac's unprecedented representation of war was the *Bulletins of the Grand Army*, a multivolume chronicle of the Napoleonic epic as a vast theater for the courage, strength and daring that make a man a man. Napoleon's personal influence was as important to the *Bulletins of the Grand Army* as to the Civil Code's provisions for making a woman a woman, a double authorial function that seems pertinent to the combination of women's and men's madness in Balzac's novella. During the two years before he wrote *Adieu*, Balzac was engaged in a long meditation on the Civil Code, especially on its representation of the sexes, and he consistently ascribed that representation to Napoleon himself. The Emperor who led Philippe and Stéphanie into Russia was for their creator the same man who imposed the statutes *enacting* their respective genders.

The single figure of Napoleon is intimately bound up with dominant ideologies of manhood and of womanhood, and the novella's separate sections combine in depicting those ideologies' uniformly disastrous effects. In Part Two as well as Part Three of *Adieu*, in war as well as in its theatrical reenactment, human beings live the consequences of invalid but hegemonic representation. In Russia as well as in France, among those consequences are intense suffering and sudden death. Stéphanie isn't the only character to be "corpsified" because representation produces a reality despite its glaring inability to reproduce one.

Realism thus confirms deconstructionist arguments that oppressive representation can have fatal consequences on those under its power. I borrowed the title of Maurice Merleau-Ponty's book *The Prose of the World* for this chapter to signal the deadening nature of existence in a society where constative reality performs existential confinement. Everything a collectivity states felicitously about gender has consequences of immense magnitude for the men and women within it.

Like speech-act theory, however, realism diverges from deconstruction by constantly proclaiming that the conventions responsible for constative effects must be understood in conjunction with the community that establishes them. For the same reason a triple "I divorce you" dissolves a marriage in some societies but not in others, a statement that a wife owes obedience to her husband can perform a fact solely through historically specific processes. Throughout the multifaceted confrontation between speech-act and post-structuralist theories to which we now turn, the central opposition is that language performs in history even though it deconstructs itself outside it.

Part III

Challenges

8

Locution, Illocution, and Deconstruction

> I consider myself to be in many respects
> quite close to Austin, both interested in and
> indebted to his problematic. (Derrida
> 1988b, p. 38)

Austin's move from locutionary identity to illocutionary force established a distinction with capital consequences for speech-act criticism of literature. In the text as well as outside it, what counts is not the structure but the performance, not the saying but the doing, not the being but the acting. As with formalist theories of language, therefore, the speech-act stance toward formalist theories of literature is simultaneously to accept and move beyond their discoveries. The characteristics of a text in itself are only one part of what enables literature to do things for, to, and with readers. The concept of textual illocution directs attention to a literary structure's interaction with the conventions governing readers' reception and interpretation of the language before them. Assessing a text's linguistic identity is for speech-act criticism one of several steps toward understanding how literature functions within the social environment where it is inevitably experienced.

As a consequence, Austinian analysis of literature bases itself on the same fundamental distinction as Austinian analysis of other forms of language, that between speech and speech acts. In the competition among critical paradigms that currently characterizes academic discourse on literature, speech-act analysis stands opposed to every vision of the text as an object, as a given and permanent entity that is what it's always been and will always remain so. Considered as *acts*, literary and non-literary utterances alike change in conjunction with the conventions they invoke and by which they are assessed. The concept of the text as static, autonomous, and determinate is radically incompatible with the Austinian vision of language as an interactive constituent of collective existence in history.

One development of formalist validation of the text as locution has been what Mary Louise Pratt called the Poetic Language Fallacy, the conviction that the text is a self-contained linguistic artifact complete unto itself. But structuralist analysis of poetic language has in recent years been broadly supplanted by the post-structuralist interpretive schemas developed from Jacques Derrida's version of deconstruction, schemas fully as concerned as speech-act criticism with textual performance and linguistic action. Like Austin, Derrida sees language as continuous transformation rather than permanent fixity. But Derrida attributes language's transformations to its triumphant *transcendence of context* whereas Austin attributes them to its inevitable *articulation with context*. The result is that speech-act theory and deconstruction have as many points of conflict as points of contact; both are vital to positioning speech-act criticism within contemporary literary theory.

As a result of Derrida's extended polemic with John Searle, the disagreements between speech-act theory and deconstruction have acquired a notoriety that has obscured the concepts on which the two philosophies stand together. Those concepts are nonetheless crucial, as many of Derrida's more intelligent commentators and disciples have taken pains to make clear. In *On Deconstruction*, for example, Jonathan Culler emphasizes Derrida's demonstration of the deconstructive moves inherent in the concept of a "supplement," simultaneously what's added to something already complete and what's needed to produce completeness. For Derrida, the "logic of supplementarity" is that by which the essential and the unessential, the outside and the inside, incessantly replace and supplant one another. Culler astutely comments on the prominence of this logic in Austin's presentation of constative and performative.

> Austin's analysis provides a splendid instance of the logic of supplementarity at work. Starting from the philosophical hierarchy that makes true or false statements the norm of language and treats other utterances as flawed statements or as extra—supplementary—forms, Austin's investigation of the qualities of the marginal case leads to a deconstruction and inversion of the hierarchy: the performative is not a flawed constative: rather, the constative is a special case of the performative. (1982, p. 113)

Undoing oppositions and reversing hierarchies figure among the most persuasively powerful strategies in deconstructive analysis, and those same strategies organize everything Austin wrote about performative and constative language.

Stanley Fish joins Culler in highlighting the Derridean overtones in Austin's devotion to dismantling the conceptual foundations he takes great care to erect.

> When all is said and done Derrida and Austin are very much alike. They are alike in writing a prose that complicates its initial assertions

and obfuscates the oppositions on which it supposedly turns; and they are alike in the use to which that prose is put, a simultaneous proffering and withdrawing of procedural tests for determining the force and significance of utterances. (1982; p. 717)

Like Shoshana Felman, Fish strongly responds to the ways Austin's style and thought are inextricably linked and exemplarily reinforcing. Austin's affinities with continental philosophers are clear in the symbiotic relationship between the organization of his prose and the strength of his ideas.

As Christopher Norris points out, this idea-style symbiosis also distances Austin's work from many of the Anglo-American philosophers who have sought to claim it for themselves: "In point of *style* [Austin's texts] are more often akin to Derrida's writings than to anything in Searle's (or Warnock's) conception of philosophical truth and authority" (1983b; p. 66). In certain areas of the Anglo-American tradition, successful philosophical writing makes itself invisible so as to provide immediate access to the majesty of the truth within it. The continental vision of language has demonstrated rather the many reasons no such invisibility is possible, and reading Austin is an uninterrupted lesson on the continental position's superiority.

As Fish points out, one consequence is that Austin's continental readers, including but not limited to Derrida, are often more open to the implications of speech-act theory than those identifying themselves as speech-act theorists.

> For Austin, the formal and the pragmatic are neither alternatives to be chosen nor simple opposites to be reconciled but the components of a dialectic that works itself out in his argument, a tacking back and forth between the commitment to intelligibility and the realization that intelligibility, although always possible, can never be reduced to the operation of a formal mechanism. That is why Derrida's reading of Austin is finally not a critique but a tribute to the radical provisionality of a text that has too often been domesticated, and it is a reading that is more faithful than many that have been offered by the master's disciples. (1982; p. 721)

The encounter between speech-act theory and deconstruction is of such interest because their disagreements over *how* language performs take off from the same constant awareness *that* it performs. Moreover, to read either Austin or Derrida is to experience language that acts out the points it's in the process of making. The "tribute" Fish reads in what Derrida presents as a critique of Austin is that of one insurgent against The Tradition and its stodginess to another.

Nonetheless, the critique is pointed, comprehensive, and weighty. "Signature Event Context," the essay in which Derrida most systematically addresses Austin's position, combines a careful laying out of deconstructive principles with a comparably careful argument that speech-act theory can't give those principles their rightful place. Although Derrida assigns suitable prominence to the distance between Austin's work and other philosophies of language, he finally classifies speech-act theory as unresponsive to the ways writing demonstrates why those philosophies are inadequate. In Derrida's view, Austin's breakaway from The Tradition is ultimately less significant than his perpetuation of its axioms on the hierarchy of writing and speech.

The epigraph to "Signature Event Context" is one of the many passages from *How to Do Things with Words* that restrict Austin's inquiry to *spoken* utterances, and Derrida immediately contests this restriction by exploring how written utterances invalidate assumptions that appear legitimate when speech alone is at issue. Philosophers have tended to conceive of language as the passive medium through which a sender communicates an intended meaning to a receiver. In the standard speech situation, sender and receiver are present together in a specific context, as the sender's intended meaning is present both in its linguistic representation and in the consciousness of the listener to whom this representation communicates. The key criterion is *presence*: speaker and listener in the presence of one another, meaning and intention present in spoken words, those words themselves present both as the physical reality of sound and the mental reality shared by the communicating parties.

In classic philosophical discourse, writing arises as a means to extend this series of presences by providing a visual representation of speech, itself the oral representation of intended meaning. But, Derrida points out, even those who conceive of writing as a direct representation of speech made for the benefit of a person not in earshot introduce a lack into a schema that ought to be characterized by wholeness. Because people write to convey a meaning to someone who isn't there, written language entails not presence but absence, an absence that is moreover not coincidental to but constitutive of writing. If written signs are the preservers of intended meaning, then that preservation has from its inception no need for the person, the subjective consciousness, that will eventually read it. "To be what it is, all writing must, therefore, be capable of functioning in the radical absence of every empirically determined receiver in general" (Derrida 1988a; p. 8). I have no way of knowing the slightest thing about those of you who will eventually read what I'm putting down, yet this writing must nevertheless remain what it is despite your absence from my current world and my current consciousness.

And when you start to think about it, you readers might have no way whatever of knowing the slightest thing about me either, and my writing *still* remains what it is. Writing, constituted by the absence of the receiver, is as a result independent of the presence of the sender. Whatever identity it has is within it, for otherwise it couldn't function as we know it does. "What holds for the receiver holds also, for the same reasons, for the sender or the producer. To write is to produce a mark that will constitute a sort of machine which is productive in turn" (8). If writing exists—and it does—it must survive unchanged regardless of what happens to the person who produces it. "For a writing to be a writing it must continue to 'act' and to be readable even when what is called the author of the writing no longer answers for what he has written" (8). I myself might be dead and gone, but the writing in front of you will function as well as if I were alive and kicking.

And doesn't this independence of producer and receiver hold for speech too? Identical to a written mark, a spoken word must be self-identical in some way wholly independent of those who speak and hear it. Otherwise it wouldn't be a spoken word. Everything that holds for writing also holds for speech; a sign of any sort must function irrespective of the empirical circumstances in which it appears. Are the characteristics of writing, Derrida asks, "limited, as is often believed, strictly to 'written' communication in the narrow sense of this word?" (10). The answer is the firmest of negatives, for what writing makes apparent holds for every conceivable form of communication. To function as a sign, a mark must possess an identity independent of those who use it and of the circumstances in which they find themselves.

Derrida's term for the self-identity requisite to every sign is "iterability," the capacity to be *repeated* by any person in any circumstances whatever without ceasing to be itself. Again writing makes apparent what's true of all signifying forms. Regardless of who you are or of where you're reading this, the words you're looking at must function in a way that repeats the identity they have here and now as I put them into the computer. In Derrida's words, unity is absolutely required for all signification, and

> this unity of the signifying form only constitutes itself by virtue of its iterability, by the possibility of its being repeated in the absence not only of its "referent," which is self-evident, but in the absence of

a determinate signified or of the intention of actual signification, as
well as of all intention of present communication. (10)

I may not give a damn about whether I communicate successfully
with you, and I may even want to mislead you in every way I possibly
can. My indifference to communication and my malicious wish to
mislead are equally irrelevant to the iterable identity of what I'm
writing, which couldn't function at all if it depended on what I want
it to be or how you see it as being.

Since spoken language must obviously also be iterable, Derrida can
use the term "graphematic" to refer to all signifying forms, oral as
well as "graphic" in the limited sense. The graphematic nature of the
sign eliminates the presence posited by standard linguistic philosophies and places a yawning absence in their place. The speaker and
listener in the presence of one another have become superfluous and
accidental. The intended meaning present in a signifying unit is irrelevant to the unit's necessarily iterable existence. The physical and
mental reality present when language is in use aren't required for
language to function, as we must recognize if we only ask ourselves
how we know which physical reality to produce when we speak and
which mental reality goes with it. Our very knowledge of what to say
when we have a certain intention shows that this knowledge must
always also be intention-free in order to be available for combining
with the intention we attach it to. Because iterability and graphematics characterize every signifying form without exception, no signifying form can depend on the inner or outer situation of the person
using it.

This outline of Derrida's argument leaves a lot out, most notably
the fact that no production of an iterable mark can ever be the exact
repetition of a previous production: to iterate is always to alter as
well as to repeat. The opening section of "Signature Event Context"
is compact and challenging, and any summary of it must introduce
distortion. Nevertheless, the categories of iterability and graphematics, along with the capacity of writing to show why they're necessary,
are the foundations of the criticisms Derrida directs at Austin. While
deconstruction assigns those categories other functions as well, my
concern here is their contribution to what is ultimately Derrida's
rejection of speech-act theory.

That contribution is immense. Derrida argues that Austin's many
insights are unsatisfactory because he ignores the graphematic nature
of every signifying form, even including a spoken form that acts.

All the difficulties encountered by Austin in an analysis which is
patient, open, aporetical, in constant transformation, often more

fruitful in the acknowledgement of its impasses than in its positions, strike me as having a common root. Austin has not taken account of what—in the structure of *locution* (thus before any illocutory or perlocutory determination)—already entails that system of predicates I call *graphematic in general*. (14)

A major consequence of Austin's failure to appreciate graphematics in general is his decision to exclude from consideration one of the most striking instances of the graphic in particular, the literary text. Derrida sees Austin's classification of literature as "parasitic" on ordinary language as an instance of the way "writing has always been treated by the philosophical tradition" (17) and therefore considers Austin's repudiation of The Tradition less consequential than his perpetuation of its refusal of graphematics.

For, as Derrida points out, what Austin considers a non-functional parasite is in fact the *sine qua non* for the life of the parasite's host, for the language used in ordinary circumstances that Austin claimed to be his only concern. If literature is a mere imitation of non-literary language, then the iterability of every signifying form means that non-literary language imitates something very like literature, as a little reflection readily shows. Assume a fully determined context identifiable as a marriage ceremony, and then ask how the officiating individual knows that the sentence with which to end the ceremony is "I now pronounce you husband and wife." Why *those* words instead of others? Why say "I now pronounce you husband and wife" rather than "Red Rover Red Rover this wedding is over" or "Ring around the roses, hold hands and rub your noses"? There's a single possible answer. The words that do things take their identity and hence their power from words that do nothing, from empty, context-free formulas that display every feature Austin identifies as beside the point. By refusing to confront the necessary iterability of every set of words, including the words that do things, Austin condemned himself to ignore the actual nature of the things words do.

Derrida chooses the interrogative mode to draw his conclusion, but the questions are tellingly declarative.

> Ultimately, isn't it true that what Austin excludes as anomaly, exception, "non-serious," *citation* (on stage, in a poem, or a soliloquy) is the determined modification of a general citationality—or rather, a general iterability—without which there would not even be a "successful" performative? [. . .] Could a performative utterance succeed if its formulation did not repeat a "coded" or iterable utterance, or in other words, if the formula I pronounce in order to open a meeting, launch a ship or a marriage were not identifiable as *conforming* with

an iterable model, if it were not then identifiable in some way as a
"citation"? (17–18)

By declaring imitation speech acts to be of no interest in analysis of
what they imitate, Derrida's Austin invalidated that analysis at its
point of departure. Iterability, the ineluctable condition of all linguistic phenomena, must be fully present in every effort to describe active
as well as inactive speech, to categorize words that do things as well
as words that remain bland and inert.

Derrida makes one other major criticism of Austin in "Signature
Event Context." Besides ignoring iterable graphematics, he contends,
speech-act theory is like other philosophies of language in requiring
a fully conscious person in control of intention and desire for its
principles to apply. Since I've extensively detailed in Chapter Five
why this critique is inapplicable to Austin however valid it may be
for other versions of speech-act theory, let me simply say here that
Derrida attaches too little importance to the "big distinction" Austin
draws between the two varieties of his six rules for performative
felicity. Whereas the four social rules are essential, the two personal
rules are incidental. Derrida mistakenly accords all six equal importance and asserts that individual intention is as crucial to Austinian
principles as collective conventions.

> [Austin] defines the six indispensable—if not sufficient—conditions
> of success. Through the values of "conventional procedure," "correct-
> ness," and "completeness," which occur in the definition, we necessar-
> ily find once more those of an exhaustively definable context, of a
> free consciousness present to the totality of the operation, and of
> absolutely meaningful speech [*vouloir-dire*] master of itself: the teleo-
> logical jurisdiction of an entire field whose organizing center remains
> *intention*. (15)

The emphasis on *intention* is Derrida's, and it runs counter to all the
many ways Austin struggles to take emphasis away from intention in
order to place it on convention: the speech "act is constituted not by
intention or by fact, essentially, but by *convention*" (Austin 1962; p.
128).

Regardless of the problem of intentionality, the fundamental dispute between Austin and Derrida is in fact over convention: what it
is, how it works, the entities to which it applies. For Austin, the
conventions that matter—those that allow speech to act—are always
socially specific and historically constituted. For Derrida, the conventions that matter apply to the units of every signifying form and thus

inhere in the nature of the mark. Since conventions inherent in the mark are obviously trans-historical and universal, Derrida's conventions are independent of context whereas Austin's are coterminous with it.

The principal manifestation of this disagreement over the conventions pertinent to speech acts is a move we've already seen, Derrida's rejection of Austin's determination to fasten on illocution, language in society, so as to show that iterability characterizes locution, language in itself. For Derrida, the general graphematics Austin fails to account for, the "common root" of all difficulties in each Austinian argument, is "in the structure of *locution* (thus before any illocutory or perlocutory determination" (14). Derrida classifies Austin's vision of speech acts as unsatisfactory because it fails to consider what speech must be before it can perform an act.

Other parts of "Signature Event Context" repeat Derrida's conviction that problems on the locutionary level must be addressed before the illocutionary level can be productively approached. An instance is this distinction between two sorts of conventionality: "Austin, at this juncture, appears to consider solely the conventionality constituting the *circumstance* of the utterance, its contextual surroundings, and not a certain conventionality intrinsic to what constitutes the locution itself" (15). Iterable graphematics characterizes any signifying mark as a signifying mark, prior to its performance in a conventional procedure with conventional effect. "Signature Event Context" consistently fastens on locution rather than illocution, Austin no less consistently on illocution rather than locution. Derrida's most sustained critique of speech-act theory is based on the nature of speech rather than the felicity of the acts it performs.

That's why the critique is nowhere near so serious as might at first appear. The abstract nature of speech is simply not pertinent to the concrete felicity of speech acts, as the abstract identity of a given locution is not pertinent to its contextual illocutionary force. To understand how and why speech acts, we must look at the *social* conventions it articulates; the trans-social conventions it also articulates are irrelevant. The words performing a marriage might indeed be "Red Rover Red Rover this wedding is over" instead of "I now pronounce you husband and wife," for no component of words' identity as words can determine their performative force as agents of society. No matter what they are in themselves, words that do things also interact with collective agreements and demand that we situate them in order to apprehend the nature of their doing. Derrida's focus on locution precludes precisely the contextualization Austin took as his special province. Iterability characterizes all signifying marks regardless of whether they function in the conventional procedures specified in Rule A.1. Austin's analysis, which begins with Rule A.1, is in no way handicapped by the intrinsic qualities of the words that do things when the rule applies. All that counts is the specific force assigned to those words by a given community's conventional procedures.

Derrida is fully justified in pointing out Austin's neglect of what constitutes locutionary identity. But it's equally justified to point out that "Signature Event Context" is almost as reticent on illocution as is *How to Do Things with Words* on locution. Austin's point of departure was *successful* illocution, words that do things regardless of the verbal or contextual factors militating against their capacity to do so. Derrida's almost exclusive concern with how such factors can make things go wrong produces a singularly schematic inquiry into the fact that they sometimes go right. In "Signature Event Context," the undecidability of every locution acquires such prominence that the effective impact of certain illocutions can be dismissed almost out of hand.

> It might be said: you cannot claim to account for the so-called graphe-matic structure of locution merely on the basis of the occurrence of failures of the performative, however real those failures may be and however effective or general their possibility. You cannot deny that there are also performatives that succeed, and one has to account for them: meetings are called to order (Paul Ricoeur did as much yesterday); people say: "I pose a question;" they bet, challenge, chris-ten ships, and sometimes even marry. It would seem that such events have occurred. And even if only one had taken place only once, we would still be obliged to account for it.
> I'll answer: "Perhaps." (17)

That "Perhaps" is the most puzzling and disconcerting component of "Signature Event Context," and I'm at a loss to understand why it's so seldom featured in the numerous commentaries on the intersections of deconstruction and speech-act theory. Derrida first lists illocutionary acts that succeed, then says even if only one succeeded it would have to be accounted for, then says it "perhaps" needs accounting for, then (in the section following the quoted passage), moves completely away from illocution to return yet again to the iterability of locution. A series of statements that felicitous speech acts do indeed occur leads not to inquiry into the social context that alone can explain how but to further consideration of the omni-contextual and trans-social features of speech in itself.

As Austin neglects graphematics and iterability, therefore, Derrida neglects performative force and illocutionary felicity. As Austin explicitly excludes literature, Derrida implicitly excludes communal interaction through and in language, even the interaction that produced the order called by Paul Ricoeur (and performed by Jacques Derrida among others) at the colloquium where "Signature Event Context" was first presented. If Austin sets what he calls non-serious utterances aside, Derrida gives serious performatives the scantest of notice.

Furthermore, the cause of both philosophers' exclusion is their concern with other matters, for Austin the place and function of language in communal existence, for Derrida the ruses and undecidability language introduces into every community. Austin's concern for illocutionary force led him to ignore the problematics of signifying form, Derrida's inquiry into the graphematics of the mark led him to classify successfully deployed illocutionary force as something that only "perhaps" calls for contemplation.

In other words, it's not that speech-act theory and deconstruction are incompatible but that they lead to different emphases, as is striking in the development Derrida gives to parallel formulations of the exigencies posed by illocution and the mark. As we saw, the statement that "even if only one [felicitous speech act] had taken place only once, we would still be obliged to account for it" leads only to "Perhaps." Contrast that reticence to the immense consequences throughout the Derridean corpus of this remark concerning the intentionless mark: "Even if this (eventual) possibility only occurred once, and never again, we would still have to account for that one time" (1988b; p. 57). That Austin and Derrida "account for" different things is a function not of different forms of blindness but of different forms of insight.

The point of consequence is that there's no compelling reason why those complementary insights can't be combined. Despite the "perhaps" in which it's collapsed, Derrida's list of felicitous illocutions makes it obvious that he's far from classifying iterable marks and performative speech as incompatible. Analogously, Austin's failure to fasten on iterable marks in no way implies that performative speech requires the self-present purity iterability precludes. Even Derrida's criticisms of speech-act theory foreground the ways Austin's vocabulary opens itself to graphematics: "So that—a paradoxical but unavoidable conclusion—a successful performative is necessarily an 'impure' performative, to adopt the word advanced later on by Austin when he acknowledges that there is no 'pure' performative" (1988a; p. 17). Rather than invalidating or contesting Austin's arguments and terminology, the concept of general iterability provides another justification for the vocabulary Austin chose and the arguments in which he applied it.

As there's no compelling reason why speech-act theory can't integrate basic deconstructive principles, there's also no reason deconstruction can't assume speech-act theory's social concerns and change "I'll say: 'Perhaps'" to "I'll say: 'Of course.'" Although the many scholars who have examined the affinities between Austin and Derrida have generally done so as a compliment to Austin, their points are just as complimentary to Derrida. Regardless of the large number of deconstructive analyses that address the timeless characteristics of discourse and ignore the historical operations to which it's applied, this emphasis is strategic not constitutive. Deconstructive incorporation of Austinian concern for the socially specific power of speech acts would broaden the strategy without contesting the methodology, as Derrida again suggests.

> By no means do I draw the conclusion that there is no relative specificity of effects of consciousness, or of effects of speech (as opposed to writing in the traditional sense), that there is no performative effect, no effect of ordinary language, no effect of presence or of discursive event (speech act). It is simply that those effects do not exclude what is generally opposed to them, term by term. (19)

"Those effects," which Austin took as his sole concern, are fully compatible with philosophical positions bringing different concerns to the fore. Speech-act theory and deconstruction have much to say to each other.

While the graphematics of the mark and the force of the performative have distinct origins, they both characterize a single entity, language put to use by the speakers of a given community. Within the terms of "Signature Event Context," all that's needed to integrate iterability and performance is awareness that, when Austin speaks of the performative's "relative purity," the adjective and the noun have equal importance. "There is a relative specificity, as Austin says, a 'relative purity' of performatives. But this relative purity does not emerge *in opposition to* citationality or iterability, but in opposition to other kinds of iteration within a general iterability" (18). The question therefore becomes the nature of the "oppositions" among different kinds of iterability, and Austinian speech-act theory gives the answer. Uniformly graphematic marks have radically different coefficients of force because of the differing conventional effects of distinct conventional procedures. What Derrida says about graphematics and what

Austin says about felicity are equally applicable to language in society. Iterability may be general, but within that generality are oppositions with vast consequences for the power of language and the lives of those who use it.

The section of "Signature Event Context" devoted to signatures repeats both Derrida's recognition of differences between marks and his relative unconcern with the social praxis constituting them. He introduces signatures as he does other performatives, by proclaiming that their undeniable reality has unmistakable impact. Then, again as with other performatives, he shifts his attention from impact to graphematics.

> Does the absolute singularity of signature as event ever occur? Are there signatures?
>
> Yes, of course, every day. Effects of signature are the most common thing in the world. But the condition of possibility of those effects is simultaneously, once again, the condition of their impossibility, of the impossibility of their rigorous purity. (20)

There follows a celebrated demonstration that the signature must be both a proof of a person's presence at a certain time and place and an infinitely repeatable mark that denies all singularity in time and space. To be recognizable as belonging to a specific individual, a signature must be identical to every other instance of the individual's handwritten name; to certify the individual's presence at a single moment, the signature must be different from every other instance of that same handwritten name. Again iterability simultaneously constructs and deconstructs language effects, and Derrida acts out his point by playing with his own handwritten name to conclude the essay he's both signing and not signing.

Absent from this play and the argument it concludes is any assertion concerning how signature effects, which Derrida calls "the most common thing in the world," have managed to become a thing in the world. The signature's iterability is undeniable. So is its force. As Jonathan Culler points out, most of us are paid by checks on which the signature is not only iterable but also a mechanical, absolutely self-identical *writing* falsely attributed to a person who never sees either the check or the "signature" that makes it payable. We nevertheless get our money. Culler and Derrida's refutations of the reasons normally adduced to explain why signatures perform neither deny that the performance is felicitous nor explore what makes it so.

Again Austinian speech-act theory has the crucial function of explaining what deconstruction leaves unexamined, the conventional procedures that allow human beings to invest a mark with force. As a locution, the signature deconstructs itself by demanding to be simultaneously repetitive and unique. As an illocution, it nevertheless does things with substantial impact on human existence. Without reliably attesting a presence, the signature still produces an effect. Austin's vision of language's role in conventional procedures explains the effect as persuasively as Derrida's concentration on graphemes eliminates the presence.

The mark's penchant for self-deconstruction in fact makes even more impressive the capacity of language communities to produce and preserve illocutionary force. Focus on social conventions, speech-act theory's great imperative, is more rather than less rewarding because the reality performed by language not only manifests collective identity but triumphs over the mark's inherent slipperiness in order to do so. Illocution, already fascinating apart from locution, is wondrous when we recognize that its effects have become the most common thing in the world despite the obstacles locution sets to their ever existing at all. Speech-act theory understands society as a dynamic process tangible in the words through which human beings interact, and deconstructive commentaries on the words enhance the fascination of the tangibility. To confront Derrida and Austin is to make both richer and more rewarding.

After two appearances in French, "Signature Event Context" first appeared in English in 1977, in the inaugural issue of *Glyph*. *Glyph* also published a highly critical response to Derrida's article by John Searle, "Reiterating the Differences: A Reply to Derrida." Derrida immediately responded to Searle with the essay called "Limited Inc abc . . .," and the polemic has gone on, most notably in Searle's 1983 review of Jonathan Culler's *On Deconstruction* in the *New York Review of Books* and Derrida's 1988 "Afterword" to the Northwestern edition of his two articles from *Glyph*.

I've found it difficult to decide the place to give the Derrida/Searle dispute in this book. On the one hand, the two philosophers' infamously hostile reactions to each other are probably what most people think of when they consider speech acts and literary theory. On the other hand, the categories around which this antagonism has expressed itself have done much to *prevent* speech-act theory from productively entering current critical debates, because those categories aren't Austin's. Searle aggressively distances himself from Austin as well as from Derrida ("I hold no brief for the details of Austin's theory of speech acts" [1977; p. 204], he says in "Reiterating the Differences"), and many of the points he raises against Derrida repudiate Austinian understanding as well. To take one example, Searle believes that his article on "The Logical Status of Fictional Discourse" gives a "detailed answer" (1977; p. 208) to all the questions Derrida raises about the relation between literary and non-literary language. As we've already seen, the absence of answers to serious literary questions in that article is concomitant with its distance from speech-act theory as Austin formulated it. Because so many of Searle's arguments are comparably hostile to the Austinian theory for which he holds no brief, the details of his polemic with Derrida are at most peripherally relevant to this book's inquiry into what Austin teaches literary critics.

So I'm going to leave aside the many points that divide Derrida and Searle for two of the points that bring them together, with Austin as well as with each other; iterability and contextual disruption of categorial purity. Searle fully acknowledges the mark's iterability and even defines it as essential to language's performative force. Although he doesn't phrase it in these terms, his point is that, because the nature of locution is without effect on the felicity of illocution, locutionary graphematics in no way deters inquiry into the things words do when they're more than locutionary.

Perhaps more importantly, Searle's polemic with Derrida leads him implicitly to abandon one of his major repudiations of Austinian principles, his assumption that speech acts are best apprehended by constructing abstract models rather than by observing concrete societies. As we saw in Chapter Four, Searle's *Speech Acts* ignores Austin's distrust of the simple situations envisaged by logical theory and defines illocution through the neat set of reliable traits provided by "a simple and idealized case" (1969; p. 56). In his review of Culler's *On Deconstruction*, Searle sets idealized simplicity aside to validate "indeterminate" phenomena that necessarily include "marginal, diverging cases" (1983b; p. 78). Searle now sees a "complex network of linguistic and social practices" that "neither require nor admit of rigorous internal boundary lines and simple mechanical methods" (79). Marginalization, indeterminacy, and complex social practices are just what *Speech Acts* sought to eliminate, and Searle's later position is incomparably closer to Austin. That's both why Derrida agrees with it (1988b; p. 155) and proof that even the bitterest disputes can be productive.

Such moments of concord among Austin, Derrida and Searle are so rare because Searle's vision of illocution sets subjective intentionality where Austin puts collective conventions. Deconstruction's encounter with every version of speech-act theory of necessity foregrounds the locution/illocution distinction. But both Searle's faith that personal intention allows illocution to perform successfully and Derrida's arguments against intentionality are irrelevant to Austin's vision of words that do things in society. This is the vision that can productively coexist with Derridean analysis of words that do things by themselves, as is best seen in the uses to which deconstructionists have put Austin's categories.

9

Performativities

Derrida concentrates on language as language, Austin on language as collective enactment of reality; one emphasizes locution, the other illocution. This distinction has had major impact on deconstructionists' understanding of verbal performativity. Because of its conviction that locution is always already problematic, Derridean analysis often represents linguistic performance as something inarticulable within speech-act parameters: a productivity intrinsic to signifying form and thus independent of communal interaction in historical time. For Austin, speech acts and illocution are synonyms, performative locution a contradiction in terms. Because Derrida understands general graphematics as activating the mark irrespective of context, he sees locution as performative independently of the conventions of Rule A.1. The concept Austin introduced to designate the force constituted by language's social position has thus been converted into a description of language without social positioning.

There is as a result a certain ambiguity when "performative" appears in deconstructive criticism. The word may designate exactly what it does for Austin, a sociolinguistic production of reality that undoes all reified understanding of the social, the linguistic, and the real. It would be hard to improve on Derrida's summary of the Austinian performative in "Signature Event Context."

> The performative does not have its referent (but here that word is certainly no longer appropriate, and this precisely is the interest of the discovery) outside of itself or, in any event, before and in front of itself. It does not describe something that exists outside of language and prior to it. It produces or transforms a situation, it effects. [This productivity] constitutes its internal structure, its manifest function or destination. (13)

Like his subsequent list of examples, Derrida's definition of the performative is totally consonant with Austin's work. On one level, there-

147

fore, speech-act theory and deconstruction are in full agreement over what it means for words to do things.

On another level, however, deconstruction introduces "performative" into arguments without connection to speech-act theory. The term can also designate language that, instead of effecting something within and outside itself at once, refuses all association with the outside to proclaim that its autonomy and self-absorption are inviolable. For Roland Barthes (1977), the best example of this kind of performativity isn't a commissive "I bet" or "I promise" but a poetic "I sing," as in Virgil's "Arms and the man I sing." The singing is in the naming of the song, the performance is felicitous by virtue of language alone, no extra-textual reality impinges on the intra-textual doing achieved when language says it's linguistic. The multiplicity of conventions in Austin's concept of speech acts is thus reduced to the single convention allowing words to name themselves as words.

This constriction of verbal performance is in obvious ways the consequence of addressing locution instead of illocution, for again the contrast is between language in and for itself and language in and for society. Although deconstructionists' *discussion* of Austin is almost always responsive to the importance of social context in his work, their *appropriation* of his terms almost always ignores social context to look at the things words do irrespective of where they are. In Austinian analysis, speech acts always perform themselves and something else as well. In deconstructive criticism, the concern has been with self-performativity alone.

One of Derrida's sustained applications of Austin's terminology occurs during the essay he called "Psyché," which analyzes a poem by Francis Ponge. The poem opens like this:

Fable
On the word *on* thus begins this text
Whose first line tells the truth.

Derrida insists on the power with which these lines, by doing and saying at once, constitute a performative exemplum. The poem *is* a fable because it *calls itself* "Fable," and its title is therefore a "poetic performative that *describes* and *effects*, on the same line, its own engendering" (1987; p. 22. All translations from "Psyché" are my own). Self-reflexive, specular performativity is stunning when the opening line of Ponge's "Fable" says nothing more than that it's producing itself as opening line: "On the word *on* thus begins this text." Though "of course not all performatives are reflexive" (22), that Ponge's text is leads Derrida to represent it as a model of performativity.

The principal reason is that the poem's mirror structure produces an instantaneously convincing demonstration that performative and constative cannot be distinguished. For a text to say that it begins on the word beginning it expresses an incontrovertible fact as well as creating an incontestable felicity; Ponge's second line says so by announcing that his first line "tells the truth." "Fable" is therefore "simultaneously *performative* and *constative* from its first line" (23). More importantly, this dual identity results not from combining two categories but from enacting each category as inevitably the other. "The statement is the performative itself since it states nothing prior or foreign to itself. It performs in stating, in effecting the statement—and nothing else" (24). Even to use Austin's two terms is misleading, for "infinitely rapid oscillation between performative and constative" (25) requires that we think both terms at once. Ponge "*on the instant* transfers performative value to the side of constative value and conversely" (24). His readers become his accomplices in radically dispersing categorial contrast. To read "Fable" is for Derrida to engage language that "spontaneously *deconstructs* the oppositional logic accepting the untouchable distinction between performative and constative and so many other associated distinctions" (25). This poem enacts itself as text by simultaneously announcing and demonstrating the radical impossibility of separating what words do from what they say.

Since Austin provides the same announcement/demonstration, since he too "spontaneously *deconstructs*" the opposition between saying and doing, we may legitimately wonder what Derrida can have in mind when he refers to the "untouchable distinction between performative and constative." Untouchable for whom? Certainly not for Austin, who takes the distinction apart with as much gusto as Ponge. The question arises again when, at the conclusion of "Psyché," Derrida says that deconstruction "continues to perturb the conditions of the performative and of that which peacefully distinguishes it from the constative" (60–61). No reader of *How to Do Things with Words* has found a peaceful distinction between performative and constative yet. Even those who, like Katz and Benveniste, want the opposition to hold are quite aware that their desire runs counter to all Austin's work. Speech-act theory perturbs the conditions of the performative as committedly as deconstruction.

But again the *causes* of the perturbation aren't the same. Austin saw logical oppositions as always possible and necessary for certain purposes even though impossible and unnecessary when the object of inquiry is language in society. Derrida sees opposition as impossible when the object is any of language's multiple varieties, and once more deconstruction orients itself toward locution prior to every illocutionary activation. Part of what "Fable" states and performs in Derrida's reading is that it has minimal need for social determination to do so. Derrida can refer to the untouchable and peaceful distinction between constative and performative because his analysis stops short of the collective dynamics that for Austin reduce the distinction to shreds.

Lecture XI of *How to Do Things with Words*, which comprehensively demonstrates the social construction of constative truth, also suggests that the basic content of the constative/performative and truth/felicity oppositions can be maintained if we rephrase them as an opposition between locution and illocution. When actually uttered, statements about the world are always also actions in the world; once produced, constatives simultaneously—*eo ipso* in Austin's donnish phrase—become performative: they constitute part of a human relationship whenever a human utters or perceives them. But we can still abstract statements from relationships and consider them solely as propositions by accepting what Austin called "an oversimplified notion of correspondence with the facts" (1962; p. 146). If we do so, it might make sense to assess a statement's truth value without concern for the conventional procedures making it an act. Although the concrete reality of illocution exists solely within those conventional procedures, the abstract meaning of locution could for Austin be imagined as existing alone.

Derrida's misleading suggestion that speech-act theory "peacefully distinguishes" performative from constative can therefore be seen as another instance of his determination to address locution alone. Ponge's "Fable" is simultaneously performative and constative because its mirror structure allows it to produce and state without needing illocutionary practices to do so. It begins on the word *on* regardless of who reads it and of the conventional context in which the reading occurs. For Derrida, its locutionary announcement of its locutionary identity means there's no need to examine its illocutionary force.

Derrida dedicates his reading of Ponge's "Fable" to Paul de Man because his own inquiry into the constative/performative breakdown continues a principal theme of de Man's critical essays. For de Man too, the locution itself—independently of collective interaction—destabilizes all contrasts between saying and doing. "The aporia between performative and constative" (de Man 1979; p. 131) is for de Man a logical self-contradiction prior to every actual or conceivable human use of language. This aporia is as a consequence disruptively present in all the actual uses of language known as texts. "A text is defined by the necessity of considering a statement, at the same time, as performative and constative [. . .] two linguistic functions which are not necessarily compatible" (270). Since deconstruction orients itself away from the communal practices Austin saw as making performative and constative not only compatible but indistinguishable, de Man presents texts as inevitably coming to grief over the very thing that lets them come to be, the assimilation of verbal action and verbal statement. Performative and constative interpenetration, for Austin the consequence of language's function in collective life, is for deconstruction one of the means by which language gets away from collective life and everything else except itself.

One reason for this deconstructionist redefinition of speech-act categories is certainly Austin's mistaken assumption that his theory had nothing to say about the "non-serious" language found in literature. Because *How to Do Things with Words* sets fiction outside its concerns, deconstructionists have assumed that their discovery of fictionality in "serious" verbal performances refutes the belief that language can actually effect the reality lived by its users. In de Man's reading of Nietzsche, for example, the contention that "the possibility for language to perform is just as fictional as the possibility for language to assert" (129) is taken as positing the impossibility for language to constitute itself as a substantial or reliable communal presence. Because Austin thought fiction wasn't serious, the fictional features in it have been taken to prove that ordinary language can't be serious either.

Barbara Johnson has pointed out that the very vocabulary Austin used to demarcate ordinary from literary language in fact deconstructs the demarcation. For Johnson, there's a huge irony in the terms that name what's left after parasitic fictions are eliminated. The lexicon Austin enlisted to say what's not imitation is a brace of words for imitation's most blatant form.

> For the very word [Austin] uses to name "mere doing," the very name he gives to that from which he excludes theatricality, is none other than the word that most commonly *names* theatricality: the word *perform*. As if this were not ironic enough, exactly the same split can be found in Austin's other favorite word: *act*. How is it that a word that expresses most simply the mere doing of an act necessarily leads us to the question of—acting? (1980; p. 65)

Johnson's Austin undermines his distinctions in the founding process of stating them for his readers. His desire to separate act from imitation produces a lexical summary of why no such separation is feasible.

But what happens if we reverse Johnson's strategy and start with the theatrical rather than the factual sense of *perform* and *act*? What if we explore the ambiguity of acting not from the impossibility of its being "mere doing" but from its concomitant inability to be mere copying? Then the duality of the words *perform* and *act* means that there's no more a space safely protected from the real world than a space safely anchored within it. Speech acts can't be named without substituting personae for persons, but personae can't be situated without the potential to function as persons. The words naming the absence of reality also name its presence.

What allows them to do so is of course their incorporation into the same social conventions that convert personae into persons, that overcome the aporia between constative and performative language to make both of them a lived collective reality. When language interacts with society, an utterance as banal as "I'm sorry" undoes logical distinctions as thoroughly as a Francis Ponge poem. Deconstructionists' refutations of Austin's opposition between literary and serious language, like their demonstration that constative and performative come together in locution as well as illocution, complicate speech-act theory without at all invalidating it. There are more reasons that Austin knew for attacking the descriptive fallacy and for bringing saying and doing together. But those reasons leave intact the vision on which speech-act theory is grounded, recognition that language performs what its users live by virtue of its articulation with the conventions they observe. Regardless of what words do as words, what they do as the agents of human coexistence remains insistently consequential. Although the performative/constative distinction can be intellectually as well as socially undone, the social practices that break it down deserve at least as much attention as the intellectual convolutions required to set it up.

I therefore find it perplexing that so few deconstructionist adaptations of Austin's terms examine the social specificity of illocutionary performance along with the trans-social undecidability of locutionary aporia. Derrida's analysis of "Fable" provocatively defines the poem as requiring "social modes of reading and reception" and "a historical configuration of poetic field and literary tradition" (38). But "Psyché" doesn't respond to its seeming call for analysis of the sociohistorical conventions that constitute textual illocution, and the poem that begins on the word *on* finally seems to bear within itself the poetic field and literary tradition also required for it to begin. The concept of language as performance, in Austin the most socialized of linguistic understandings, has been for deconstruction another way to extract language from society.

A spectacular example is de Man's interpretation of the passage in Rousseau's *Confessions* that narrates the young Jean-Jacques's theft of a ribbon and his denunciation of Marion, a fellow servant, as the actual thief. De Man concentrates on the many passages in the *Confessions* where Rousseau insists he had no desire to harm Marion when he named her as the person who gave him the stolen ribbon. Quite the contrary: because he had warm, friendly feelings toward Marion, Rousseau was thinking of her when accused of the theft; because he was thinking of Marion, hers was the name ready at hand when he sought to defend himself against the accusation. "I excused myself on the first thing that offered itself"; because Rousseau cared for Marion and had her in his thoughts, the first thing that offered itself was her name.

For de Man, Rousseau's statement that he excused himself on the first thing available is "the key sentence in the *Confessions*" (1979; p. 292) because it alienates language from the two grounding certainties traditionally ascribed to it, referential accuracy and speaker's intention. To excuse oneself is a classic performative, and its felicity is therefore conventionally rather than referentially established. What de Man calls "the performative power of the lie as excuse" (291) is indistinguishable from the performative power of the truth as excuse, for when speech is active the true/false distinction doesn't apply. As "I guess the window's open" is a guess regardless of the window's condition, Rousseau's "Marion" is an excuse regardless of her innocence. Her name "stands entirely out of the system of truth" (289) because the system that applies is performative not cognitive.

Moreover, "Marion" stands apart from the intentions of the man who said it as well as the acts of the woman it accused. De Man, attaching huge importance to Rousseau's insistence that he had no wish to harm, posits "a complete disjunction between Rousseau's desires and interests and the selection of this particular name" (288). That disjunction means that we have no more right to attach meaning and reference to "Marion" than to attribute malice to Rousseau, and for de Man standard linguistic understandings become suddenly inapplicable. "The estrangement between subject and utterance is then so radical that it escapes any mode of comprehension" (289). Not only does language fail to express intention, it fails to express anything whatever. "Rousseau was making whatever noise happened to come into his head; he was saying nothing at all, least of all someone's name" (292). De Man understands "Marion" as a pure locution, without connection to the man who said it, to the woman it named, to the world where man and woman lived.

This reading, among the most celebrated deconstructionist applications of speech-act categories, is also among the most informative on what puts the Austinian and Derridean visions of language together and apart. De Man's demonstration of the discontinuity between Rousseau's will and his "Marion" illustrates Austin's argument against the "quite mistaken" view that speech acts are "the outward and visible sign [. . .] of an inward and spiritual act" (Austin 1962; p. 9). Rousseau's inward and spiritual disposition militated *against* his saying anything that would hurt Marion, and one part of de Man's reading of Rousseau directly develops his reading of Austin.

Yet de Man and Austin's common repudiation of the intentional and descriptive fallacies is far less consequential than their contrary validations of locution and illocution, which raise powerful objections to the entire deconstructive focus on language apart from and prior to its social actualization. De Man reads the end of language's responsibility for descriptive accuracy and intentional expression as its total liberation from everything except itself. Because Rousseau "was saying nothing at all," for de Man he wasn't doing anything at all either. His locution had no illocutionary value.

In Austin's work, however, repudiation of the descriptive and intentional fallacies is one step toward *revealing* language's illocutionary value as the vehicle/agent of collective conventions. That Rousseau was saying nothing at all is therefore quite irrelevant to the vileness of what his speech act was doing: slandering an innocent person, causing her dismissal with prejudice from her position, and in all probability destroying her life. What Austin insisted so fervently for the promise is at least as valid for the calumny: it doesn't make a damned bit of difference whether you meant what you said, what counts is the thing you did when you said it. The thing Rousseau did was despicable. The failure of intentional or referential visions of language to explain why makes the straightforward speech-act explanation all the more important. De Man assumes that language's disjunction from intention makes it a free-floating form without external connections, that the radical estrangement between subject and utterance "escapes any mode of comprehension" (289). For Austin, this estrangement leads not away from but toward comprehension, toward recognition that language enacts human commitments to other humans. The failure to respect those commitments in Rousseau's slander compellingly displays why Austinian comprehension is necessary.

According to de Man, if Marion's "nominal presence is a mere coincidence, then we are entering an entirely different system" (289). This new, purely locutionary system is one in which the "absolute randomness of language" (299) means that it and its speakers are forever free of accountability for what it does. The contrast with Austin couldn't be greater. Speech-act theory accepts the possibility of nominal presence being a mere coincidence in order to foreground speaker's immense accountability for the names they perform with or without motivation. That Marion's name is an *intentional* coincidence has no pertinence to the *conventional* act accomplished in Rousseau's utterance of it, an act at least as reprehensible in the absence of ill will as it would be with malice aforethought.

The Austinian category of locution is an abstraction, a means of designating an entity that, like Saussure's "language" and Chomsky's "competence," can be thought but can't be produced: "To perform a locutionary act is in general, we may say, also and *eo ipso* to perform an *illocutionary* act" (Austin 1962, p. 98). Whenever uttered in historical time, which is to say whenever uttered, locution inevitably becomes the sign and performance of conventional procedures. Rousseau's "Marion" memorably illustrates why language used is always illocution performed. Agreed he meant no harm, agreed his utterance had no referential value; it nevertheless had such crushing illocutionary force that de Man's perception of it as a pure locution becomes almost incomprehensible.

In this "Marion," the conventions activating language and activated by it are unmistakable. A form of court proceeding is underway, everything said is perceived by all those present (certainly including Rousseau) as something done as well. If ever a contextual situation has made words' illocutionary status obvious, this is it. And yet de Man's concentration on locution leads him to see almost nothing of interest in the devastating act performed by Rousseau's word.

Almost nothing instead of nothing at all: de Man of course recognizes the injury done to Marion, but he contends that the culprit is not Rousseau, who simply produced a pure locution. The harm was done by those who took what Rousseau said as illocutionary, who believed that language produced during a conventional procedure should be understood according to the rules the procedure imposes. De Man so decontextualizes "Marion" as to blame what it did on those who understood it in context, the judges who heard Rousseau say Marion gave him the ribbon and took the statement to be consonant with the conventions being performed.

> Not the fiction itself is to blame for the consequences but its falsely referential reading. As a fiction, the statement is innocuous and the error harmless; it is the misguided reading of the error as theft or slander, the refusal to admit that fiction is fiction, the stubborn resistance to the "fact," obvious by itself, that language is entirely

free with regard to referential meaning and can posit whatever its grammar allows it to say, which leads to the transformation of random error into injustice. (293)

All Austin's work stands opposed to the consequences de Man here draws from the fact that "language is entirely free with regard to referential meaning and can posit whatever its grammar allows it to say." It's *because* of this freedom of language in itself that societies require and empower words to perform the agreements their members have with each other. To attribute the harm done by violation of commitments to those who maintained conventions as established is a violent expropriation of Austin's categories from the founding conditions specified in Rule A.1.

Everything de Man says about language in his essay on Rousseau's excuse is valid for locution, nothing he says about language acknowledges the reality of illocution. This binary contrast is so pervasive that de Man not only blames the injustice to Marion on those who recognize illocutionary force as forceful but even castigates their "stubborn resistance" to seeing language as pure locution. "If the essential non-signification of the statement had been properly interpreted" (292), he argues, no harm would have been done. The implication is that "properly interpreted" language is always detached from speakers' social situation. The force of Rousseau's slander illustrates why speech-act analysis considers this detachment to produce the most improper interpretation of all.

Given the prominent deconstructionist antagonism to the concepts of "proper" and "propriety," it's probably wrong to attach deep thematic import to de Man's call for "properly interpreted" language. As deconstruction has taught us, however, unintentional slips are often the most revealing of all speech acts, and it's interesting to note the ways de Man's interpretive operations simply reverse the intentionalist and referential assumptions that also set proper interpretation atop their list of priorities. Once those assumptions are overturned, de Man contends, there can be no meaning at all, and proper understanding comes from recognizing that every appearance of meaning is an illusion asking to be taken apart.

For Austin, however, eliminating the intentionalist and descriptive fallacies doesn't destroy meaning but opens the way to understand its constitution by and of the protocols organizing collective interaction. That those protocols can always be. violated, that language can be both abstracted from conventions and used in ways they prohibit, in no way threatens the social reality of language used and interpreted

according to the conventional procedures observed by a given community. Despite its referential failure, despite its estrangement from
Rousseau's will and intention, "Marion" was fully meaningful for the
same reason it was fully active: it was integrated into a conventional
procedure with baleful conventional effect.

For the descriptive fallacy, proper names are nothing but the labels
of the persons that bear them. De Man's deconstructionist reading of
Rousseau upends this assumption and collapses the person Marion
into the sign "Marion." The lady vanishes; her name becomes her only
reality. "Marion just happened to be the first thing that came to mind;
any other name, any other word, any other sound or noise could have
done just as well and Marion's entry into the discourse is a mere effect
of chance. She is a free signifier" (288). Because de Man's essay uses
quotation marks when the name "Marion" is to be taken as a sign, the
absence of quotation marks here puts the person into discourse and
out of existence. It's not just that Marion's *name* is a free signifier.
"*She* is a free signifier," indistinguishable in de Man's rhetoric from
"any other word, any other sound or noise." The descriptive fallacy's
elimination of signs for referents has been replaced by elimination of
referents for signs, and the unpleasantness of choosing between the
two is why speech-act theory has so much to offer the current critical
scene. Language is active not passive, but the way it acts is of far more
than locutionary concern. Austin's vision of verbal performance is the
best explanation of why Marion and "Marion" must be apprehended
together for either to be "properly interpreted."

Of the many critical reactions to de Man's essay on the Marion
episode, the one of greatest pertinence here is Steven Knapp and
Walter Benn Michaels's "Against Theory." This essay, based on John
Searle's belief that intention is the ground of illocutionary force, argues that intentions also ground language as a whole. Knapp and
Michaels believe that intentionless language isn't really language at
all. De Man was consequently wrong to see "Marion" as linguistic; the
word couldn't be a word because it wasn't intentional.

> De Man's mistake is to think that the sound "Marion" remains a
> signifier even when emptied of all meaning. The fact is that the
> meaningless noise "Marion" only *resembles* the signifier "Marion,"
> just as accidentally uttering the sound "Marion" only *resembles* the
> speech act of naming Marion. De Man recognizes that the accidental
> emission of the sound "Marion" is not a speech act (indeed, that's the
> point of the example), but he fails to recognize that it's not language
> either. What reduces the signifier to noise and the speech act to an
> accident is the absence of intention. (23)

Knapp and Michaels find the Austinian category of locution meaningless. Either language is intentional or it isn't language but rather "noise" and "accident."

Exactly like de Man, however, Knapp and Michaels are indifferent to the crushing act performed by the intentionless "Marion." Although denunciation is a clear example of the things done by words, although the things done here were done to an innocent person as well as by an articulated sound, Knapp and Michaels's commitment to Searle's validation of intentionality convinces them that "the sound 'Marion' is not a speech act." The failure of the intentionalist schema even to perceive the action in Rousseau's slander demonstrates what's lost when Searle is substituted for Austin.

As the title "Against Theory" suggests, Knapp and Michaels argue that every theoretical approach to literary criticism is misguided and useless; they want criticism simply to recognize that texts say what they mean and mean what they say. In direct contrast, de Man's version of deconstruction is among the most theoretically sophisticated critical positions of recent decades. De Man has shown time and again why it's impossible for texts simply to say what they mean, why it's naive for a critic to assume that they mean what they say. It's remarkable that these diametrically opposed critical perspectives agree that Rousseau's "Marion" is not a speech act. You'd think a critical method that failed to see anything real in the calumny of an innocent woman by a guilty man would be abandoned for that reason alone. Yet both the deconstructionist and the intentionalists see no problem at all in their methodology's failure to perceive a speech act where speech is blatantly active.

An analogous privileging of critical principles over linguistic action can produce a lack of concern for the illocutionary force of texts in general. According to anti-theoretical intentionalists, a literary work's interaction with the social conventions observed by its readers doesn't count if the work's author didn't mean for it to occur. For hyper-theoretical deconstructionists, the historical facts constituted by textual illocution are less interesting than the locutionary quandaries that problematize the assumptions normally advanced to explain the factuality in process.

Austinian criticism corrects both errors. Even if language is, as de Man believes, "radically formal, i. e. mechanical" (1979; p. 294), it's also radically social, i. e. performative; criticism can and should investigate the consequences. Even if the author didn't mean a work to act the way it does, there's no justification for critics to believe the action isn't there because it's really a void that, in Knapp and Michaels's emphatic terms, "only *resembles* the speech act." Whether in or out of texts, language does things that matter, and Austin's work is an immense aid to understanding why and how.

Nowhere is Austin's work more gripping than when applied to revolutionary situations in which the things done by words have world-historical consequences. In his analysis of the American Declaration of Independence, Derrida pays eloquent homage to the ways an Austinian perspective on historical upheaval dismantles classic understandings of representation while preserving full respect for the impact of representational action. At the same time, Derrida sees even in revolutionary declarations a nostalgia for presence that finally strives to insulate the constative from the performative, and his conclusion is that revolution cannot escape the standard aporia of Western philosophy and politics. The two names for the two moves in Derrida's reading of the Declaration of Independence are "the American people" and "God." I'll hold God off and begin with the American people.

The problem confronting the delegates to Philadelphia in the summer of 1776 was that they also had to begin with the American people even though there could be no such people until the delegates had ended what they were to begin. Their quandary was implicit in their names for themselves and their achievement: "We, therefore, the representatives of the United States of America in General Congress assembled, do in the name and by the authority of the good people of these [. . .] free and independent States." When that statement was written, there was no United States of America, no General Congress assembled, no free and independent states, no good people in whose name and by whose authority the General Congress could act. It was through speaking in the name of the American people that the delegates produced a people to name; it was by invoking an authority that they established an authority to invoke.

But at the same time, the people must already have existed for its representatives to gather together. National authority must by definition have preceded its invocation and application. As Derrida says, the signature invents the signer who patently had to have been already invented before signing. "We cannot determine, and all the interest is in this, the force and the *coup de force* of such a declarative act, whether independence is *stated* or *produced* by this utterance [. . .] This obscurity, this undecidability between, let us say, a performative structure and a constative structure, are *required* to produce the effect sought [. . .] By signing, the people say—and do what they say they are doing" (1984; pp. 20–22. All translations from Derrida's analysis of the Declaration of Independence are my own). This positive effect of a simultaneously performative and constative declaration has of course a negative consequence, dissolution of a colonial government that, by *not* being spoken, ceased to exist in no less decisive a fashion than a General Congress and a good people came to be. In the negative case, a referent fails to produce a sign and thus ceases to be a referent. In the positive case, a sign performs without a referent and thereby acquires daunting referential presence. In both cases, the hierarchy and symbiosis of referent and sign in classic representational thought are discombobulated as the Austinian speech act produces what it says by virtue of performing as if the production had already occurred.

Derrida is appropriately enthusiastic about the explanatory richness of Austin's categories in describing transformational events like the American Revolution. As in "Signature Event Context," his critique comes only after a detailed appreciation of the achievement he means to criticize. In the Declaration of Independence, that achievement—the performative production of a nation that is also the constative guarantee of the language establishing it—is for Derrida vitiated by language that claims entitlement by the ultimate authority the Declaration of Independence refers to as Nature and Nature's God. The assembly "signs in the name of the laws of nature and in the name of God. It *poses* its institutional laws on the foundation of natural laws [. . .] and in the name of God, the creator of nature [. . .] He founds natural laws and therefore the whole game tending to present performative utterances *as* constative utterances" (25).

It's only after appealing to the "Supreme Judge of the World" that the revolutionary delegates make their ultimate statement "in the Name and by the Authority of the good People" and "solemnly publish and declare that these united Colonies are and of right ought to be free and independent states." Derrida's explication of such language posits a group of delegates in total regression from knowledge that their connection to the people and the nation meant that they needed no referent before making reference to it.

> "Are and ought to be:" the "and" here articulates and conjoins the two discursive modalities, is and ought-to-be, statement and prescription, fact and right. *And* is God [. . .] For this Declaration to have a sense *and* an effect, there must be a last instance. God is the name, the best one, for this last instance and this ultimate signature. (27–28)

Derrida's celebration of the absolute undecidability of constative and performative prepares his condemnation of language that appears to affirm belief in an unproblematically decidable referent outside and prior to itself. There was no American people before its existence was declared and performed, but the appeal to Nature and Nature's God completely undoes the liberating thrust of the speech act it accompanies. In Derrida's regretful rhetoric, "And yet. And yet another instance is waiting behind the scenes. Another 'subjectivity' comes in to sign, in order to guarantee it, this signature production" (24). The name of God, the proper name of God, acts apart from speech to accredit and thus discredit the speech acts performing a nation both present and absent in the name given it.

From one point of view, Derrida has every reason to distinguish so aggressively between the United States of America, which came into being on July 4, 1776, and Nature, Nature's God, and the laws common to both, which had always been and would always be. One is obviously a historically specific creation of speech and acts, the others no less obviously eternal beings unaffected by the speech and acts unfolding in historical time. And yet. And yet positing any such distinction does clear violence to Austin's assimilation of constative and performative language, his most stimulating insight into the course of human events. Because the constative is a subcategory of the performative, the qualities the constative states are always qualities performed even when—especially when—what is stated is that performance is unnecessary. The ahistorical permanence of Nature and Nature's God isn't a given fact but a collectively validated convention enacted in language. Like a nation's form of government, its God exists by virtue of communal affirmation through speech and acts. The definition of the existence communally affirmed, whether it is posited as eternal or as beginning here and now, is without interest. The Declaration of Independence *performed* both God and the United States of America, and the fact that the performance was explicit in one case and implicit in the other is trivial.

Revolutions always do at least two things. They demonstrate the historically transient character of the course of human events, and they claim to set history on the track it should have followed from the beginning of time. The first necessarily involves an overt display that constative and performative cannot be separated, but the second requires holding constative truth to be self-evident and hence independent of performance. The perspective ultimately established in *How to Do Things with Words* demands that, in opposition to Derrida's procedure, we see this distinction as itself a performance, that we recognize the identity of referents produced and referents affirmed, of history and eternity, of a congress newly assembled and Nature's timeless God. All are the effect of collective action and collective speech, each of which must entail the other if reference is to occur.

For Derrida, God's introduction into the writings of the Continental Congress denied those writings' graphematic identity: "The Congress *poses* its institutional laws on the foundations of natural laws." For speech-act theory, on the contrary, the foundations furnished by natural laws are no less the conventional effect of a conventional procedure than the institutional laws those foundations support. Both display simultaneously the vertiginous iterability of graphematics and the transformational solidity of historically determinate and historically determinant action. Both simultaneously overturn and displace a conceptual order and affirm and reorganize the non-conceptual order with which it is articulated.

And the Declaration of Independence could be both graphematic and transformational solely because the articulation of conceptual and non-conceptual orders was such as to make a revolution. Derrida talks about the verbal performance of the United States without a single allusion to the non-verbal rebellion that allowed the performance to be held over. Yet absolutely nothing in the *text* of the Declaration of Independence—in its identity as *locution*—allows it to institute the nation it names.

The undecidability between a performative structure and a constative structure, the unanswerable question of whether independence was *stated* or *produced*, inheres solely in the fact that independence was acquired, that the good people of the United States of America came to be through coming to be spoken. Absent independence, a declaration of independence is not in the least an undecidable oscillation between performative and constative. Imagine the text of July 4, 1776, if all rebellious forces had surrendered on July 5, 1776. The words would be the same, but they would be pure iteration without performance, pure textual play without pragmatic force. That they have the potential to do nothing is of interest but not of moment in an Austinian explanation of how they actualized their potential to do something.

How did this actualization occur? The same way every speech act becomes felicitous, through the *illocutionary* interaction of language and reality that makes language real and reality linguistic at the same time. The United States of America came into being through and in the words of the Declaration of Independence, but to understand why we must look at the historical context that made those words an act—while itself being performed as historical context by those same words. We can neither derive the Declaration of Independence from the War of Independence nor understand the words of the Declaration apart from the collective dynamics also active in the events of the

War. Identical to a promise or a bet, the General Congress of the United States of America became at once a verbal sign and a referential fact on July 4, 1776. It performed and named itself in a single move, and every such sociolinguistic production is constitutively related to the circumstances effected and accepted by those among whom it counts as valid.

There's a crucial distinction between the Declaration of Independence and Francis Ponge's "Fable," the two texts to which Derrida applies speech-act categories. Ponge's language makes itself simultaneously performative and constative by saying what it's doing; Jefferson's leaves the doing unexpressed. Context alone reveals that the Declaration's articulation of the General Congress also produced it; this language is creation only for those who know that what was named didn't exist before the naming occurred. Whereas Ponge's "On the word *on* thus begins this text" is both performative and constative to every reader, Jefferson's "representatives of the United States of America in General Congress assembled" can appear to be a classic constative if readers are unaware of its historical context.

Derrida's insistence that Jefferson's language is both statement and production is therefore thoroughly historicized, for it depends on the fact that the independence produced couldn't have been simply stated because it wasn't there. Rather than exploit this historical foundation of his analysis, however, Derrida argues that the Declaration of Independence is in fact identical to "Fable." He sees the new nation's authorization of its own authority not as a historical speech act but as a "fabulous retroactivity" (22) strongly reminiscent of the fabulous mirror structure in "Fable." The implication is that Jefferson's text is, like Ponge's, simultaneously performative and constative not because it's an illocution in productive collaboration with collective will but because it too is a locution collaborating solely with itself.

In Derrida's representation, the good people of the United States of America guarantee the truth of their name, this name performs the good people, for the same reason the first line of "Fable" tells the truth. "There was no rightful signer before the text of the Declaration, which itself remains the producer and guarantor of its own signature. By this fabulous event, by this fable that implies the trace and is actually possible only through the inadequation to itself of a present, a signature gives itself a name" (23). Again the lived reality of illocution, here the inaugural performance of the United States of America, disappears for the problematics of locution, the "inadequation to itself of a present." The world-historical impact of a speech act overcoming the aporia of speech is mentioned only to be dropped. Deconstruction, which furnishes a powerful means for explaining what "Fable" and the Declaration of Independence have in common, is almost silent on the social context that makes the two *do* such different things.

That's why it's essential to recognize the complementarity of speech-act theory and deconstruction. The two interpretive methods share the determination to erase the boundary lines between literary and non-literary utterance, but the erasures have different motivations. Deconstruction foregrounds the *locutionary perplexities* common to literary and non-literary utterances, speech-act theory their common *illocutionary activity*. One method concentrates on the things language does by virtue of its nature, the other on the things it does by virtue of its conventional context. Where deconstruction assimilates non-literary language like that in the Declaration of Independence to the self-contained artifacts constituted by poems like "Fable," speech-act theory sees poems like "Fable" as situated in time and space no less firmly than historical documents like the Declaration of Independence. Austinian analysis is in fact a perfect response to Derrida's call for attention to poetry's dependence on "social modes of reading and reception" and on the "historical configuration" of every literary field (Derrida 1987; p. 38). Because of its own concentration on locution, by definition above the historical configuration of social modes of reading, deconstruction itself has yet to establish the paradigms for socialized linguistic analysis that are speech-act criticism's point of departure.

Paul de Man's description of Rousseau's "Marion" employs terms reminiscent of deconstructive criticism's approach to far lengthier texts. Emphasis in both cases falls on the fact that language's disconnection from subjective intention and objective truth mean that it is "entirely free [. . .] and can posit whatever its grammar allows it to say" (de Man 1979; p. 293). Speech-act theory, without contesting this point either for the text or for Rousseau's denunciation, nevertheless argues that—in both the text and the denunciation—the utterances allowed by a language's grammar also enact the interrelationships of its speakers.

Despite its persuasive challenges to so many structuralist presuppositions, deconstruction finally diverges from speech-act theory in the same way as structuralism, by choosing to address locution rather than illocution. In "Signature Event Context," Derrida rejects Austin's concern with "the conventionality constituting the *circumstances* of the utterance, its contextual surroundings" (1988a; p. 15). His own focus is the conventionality displayed by language regardless of its circumstances and surroundings. Deconstruction and speech-act theory have different visions of performativity because one sets language within the relations lived by its users while the other addresses language in and for itself.

The speech-act theorist's imperative is to concentrate on language's illocutionary force, the deconstructionist's to address the performativity "intrinsic to what constitutes the locution itself" (Derrida 1988a; p. 15). De Man's essay on Rousseau's *Confessions* is a memorable instance of exclusive attention to intrinsic properties annihilating extrinsic circumstances, and the result is that Rousseau's stunningly powerful speech act becomes an empty signifier, that illocution becomes locution. De Man brackets context and circumstances to represent language as unconstrained by anything other than the locutionary properties that constitute its grammar. Speech-act theory sets social protocols at the center of its vision of linguistic performativity, deconstruction sets them aside.

This book therefore ends as it began, by asserting that speech-act theory's concern for the *social* process of verbal performativity is unique among contemporary critical schools. For Austinian analysis, the text actively participates in the sociohistorical dynamics of conventional interaction. The principal tenets of speech-act criticism are that language in society invariably enacts collective life and that literature is invariably language in society.

Bibliography

Austin, J. L. (1961) *Philosophical Papers*. Oxford, Oxford UP.

Austin, J. L. (1962) *How to Do Things with Words*. Cambridge, Harvard UP.

Austin, J. L. (1971) "Performative-Constative." In John R. Searle, ed. *The Philosophy of Language*. Oxford, Oxford UP, pp. 13–22.

Avni, Ora (1983) "A Bicêtre: Austin, Searle, Nerval." *MLN* 98(4), pp. 624–638.

de Balzac, Honoré (1974) *Adieu*. In *Le Colonel Chabert suivi de Trois Nouvelles*. Paris, Folio, pp. 145–216.

Baron, Dennis E. (1975) "Role Structure and the Language of Literature." *Journal of Literary Semantics* 4, pp. 43–51.

Barthes, Roland (1977) "The Death of the Author." In his *Image, Music, Text*. New York, Hill and Wang, pp. 142–148.

Bauerlein, Mark (1986) "The Written Orator in 'Song of Myself:' A Recent Trend in Whitman Criticism." *Walt Whitman Quarterly Review* 3(3), pp. 1–14.

Beardsley, Monroe C. (1973) "The Concept of Literature." In Frank Brady, John Palmer, and Martin Price, eds. *Literary Theory and Structure*. New Haven and London, Yale UP, pp. 23–39.

Beardsley, Monroe C. (1978) "Aesthetic Intentions and Fictive Illocutions." In Paul Hernadi, ed. *What is Literature?* Bloomington, Indiana UP, pp. 161–177.

Benveniste, Emile (1971) "Analytical Philosophy and Language." In his *Problems of General Linguistics*, tr. M. E. Meeks. Coral Gables, University of Miami Press, vol. 1, pp. 231–238.

Berlin, Isaiah et al. (1973) *Essays on J. L. Austin*. Oxford, Clarendon Press.

Brown, Robert L. and Martin Steinmann (1978) "Native Readers of Fiction: A Speech-Act and Genre-Rule Approach to Defining Literature." In Paul Hernadi, ed. *What is Literature?* Bloomington, Indiana UP, pp. 141–160.

Burke, Kenneth (1975) "Words as Deeds." *Centrum* 3(2), pp. 147–168.

Campbell, B. G. (1975) "Toward a Workable Taxonomy of Illocutionary Forces, and its Implication to Works of Imaginative Literature." *Language and Style* 8(1), pp. 3–20.

Cavell, Stanley (1979) "Austin and Examples." In his *The Claim of Reason.* Oxford, Clarendon Press, pp. 49–64.

Cavell, Stanley (1982) "Politics as Opposed to What?" *Critical Inquiry* 9(1), pp. 157–178.

Chambers, Ross (1980) "Le masque et le miroir: Vers une théorie relationnelle du théâtre." *Etudes littéraires* 13(3), pp. 397–412.

Chatman, Seymour (1975) "The Structure of Narrative Transmission." In Roger Fowler, ed. *Style and Structure in Literature.* Ithaca, Cornell UP, pp. 213–257.

Culler, Jonathan (1982) *On Deconstruction: Theory and Criticism after Structuralism.* Ithaca, Cornell UP.

de Man, Paul (1979) *Allegories of Reading: Figural Language in Rousseau, Nietzsche, Rilke and Proust.* New Haven and London, Yale UP.

Derrida, Jacques (1984) "Déclarations d'Indépendance." In his *Otobiographies.* Paris, Galilée, pp. 13–32.

Derrida, Jacques (1987) "Psyché: Invention de l'Autre." In his *Psyché.* Paris, Galilée, pp. 11–61.

Derrida, Jacques (1988a) "Signature Event Context." In his *Limited Inc.* Evanston: Northwestern UP, pp. 1–23.

Derrida, Jacques (1988b) *Limited Inc.* Evanston, Northwestern UP.

Ducrot, Oswald. (1972) "De Saussure à la philosophie de langage." Preface to Searle, *Les Actes de Langage.* Paris, Hermann, pp. 7–34.

Elam, Keir. (1980) *The Semiotics of Theatre and Drama.* London and New York, Methuen.

Elam, Keir. (1984) *Shakespeare's Universe of Discourse.* Cambridge, Cambridge UP.

Fanto, James A. (1978) "Speech-Act Theory and its Applications to the Study of Literature." In R. W. Bailey, L. Matejka, and P. Steiner, eds. *The Sign: Semiotics around the World.* Ann Arbor, Michigan Slavic Publications, pp. 280–304.

Felman, Shoshana (1975) "Women and Madness: The Critical Phallacy." *Diacritics* 5(4), pp. 2–10.

Felman, Shoshana (1983) *The Literary Speech Act: Don Juan with Austin, or Seduction in Two Languages.* Tr. Catherine Porter. Ithaca, Cornell UP.

Fish, Stanley (1980) "How to Do Things with Austin and Searle: Speech-Act Theory and Literary Criticism." In his *Is There a Text in this Class?* Cambridge, Harvard UP, pp. 197–245.

Fish, Stanley (1982) "With the Compliments of the Author: Reflections on Austin and Derrida." *Critical Inquiry* 8, pp. 693–721.

Gann, Myra (1986) "The Performative Status of Verbal Offenses in *A secreto agravio, secreta venganza.*" In Rivers (1986), pp. 39–49.

Gascar, Pierre (1974) "Préface" to Balzac (1974), pp. 7–18.

Hancher, Michael (ed.) (1975a) "Discussion" of the Midwest MLA forum on "Speech Acts and Literature." *Centrum* 3(2), pp. 125–146.

Hancher, Michael (1975b) "Understanding Poetic Speech Acts." *College English* 36, pp. 632–639.

Hancher, Michael (1977) "Beyond a Speech-Act Theory of Literary Discourse." *MLN* 92, pp. 1081–1098.

Hancher, Michael (1979) "The Classification of Cooperative Illocutionary Acts." *Language in Society* 8, pp. 1–14.

Harré, R. (1983) "Language and Social Action." In Roy Harris, ed. *Approaches to Language*. Oxford, Pergamon Press, pp. 127–141.

Hirsch, E. D. (1975) "What's the Use of Speech-Act Theory?" *Centrum* 3(2) pp. 121–124.

Holdcroft, David (1983) "Irony as a Trope, and Irony as Discourse." *Poetics Today* 4(3), pp. 493–511.

Hollis, C. Carroll (1983) "Speech Acts and *Leaves of Grass.*" In his *Language and Style in "Leaves of Grass"*. Baton Rouge, Louisiana State UP, pp. 65–123.

Iser, Wolfgang (1975) "The Reality of Fiction: A Functionalist Approach to Literature." *New Literary History* 7(1), pp. 7–38.

Johnson, Barbara (1980) "Poetry and Performative Language: Mallarmé and Austin." In her *The Critical Difference*. Baltimore, Johns Hopkins UP, pp. 52–66.

Kamuf, Peggy (1988) "Floating Authorship." In her *Signature Pieces: On the Institutution of Authorship*. Ithaca, Cornell UP, pp. 177–200.

Katz, Jerrold (1977) *Propositional Structure and Illocutionary Force*. Sussex, Harvester Press.

Knapp, Steven and Walter Benn Michaels (1985) "Against Theory." In W. J. T. Mitchell, ed. *Against Theory: Literary Studies and the New Pragmatism*. Chicago, University of Chicago Press, pp. 11–30.

Kuhns, Richard (1978) " 'Performatives' in Linguistic Art." *Centrum* 6(2) pp. 113–117.

Levenston, Edward A. (1976) "Metaphor, Speech Act and Grammatical Form." *Poetics* 5, pp. 373–381.

Levin, Samuel R. (1976) "Concerning What Kind of Speech Act a Poem Is." In Teun A. van Dijk, ed. *Pragmatics of Language and Literature*. Amsterdam, North Holland, pp. 141–160.

Mack, Dorothy (1975) "Metaphoring as Speech Act: Some Happiness Conditions for Implicit Similes and Simple Metaphors." *Poetics* 4, pp. 221–256.

Maclean, Ian (1985) "Un Dialogue de Sourds? Some Implications of the Austin-Searle-Derrida Debate." *Paragraph* 5, pp. 1–26.

Marlowe, Christopher (1986) *The Complete Plays.* London, Penguin.

Martland, T. R. (1978a) "What Does it Mean to Say Literature Represents 'Nothing'?" *Centrum* 6(2), pp. 104–112.

Martland, T. R. (1978b) "Response." *Centrum* 6(2), pp. 128–132.

Norris, Christopher (1983a) "Deconstruction and 'Ordinary Language:' Speech versus Writing in the Text of Philosophy." In his *The Deconstructive Turn.* London and New York, Methuen, pp. 13–33.

Norris, Christopher (1983b) " 'That the Truest Philosophy is the Most Feigning': Austin and the Margins of Literature." In his *The Deconstructive Turn.* London and New York, Methuen, pp. 59–84.

Norris, Christopher (1985) "Suspended Sentences: Textual Theory and the Law." *Southern Review* 18(2), pp. 123–141.

Norris, Christopher (1986) "Home Thoughts from Abroad: Derrida, Austin and the Oxford Connection." *Philosophy and Literature* 10(1), pp. 1–25.

Ohmann, Richard (1971a) "Speech Acts and the Definition of Literature." *Philosophy and Rhetoric* 4, pp. 1–19.

Ohmann, Richard (1971b) "Speech, Action and Style." In Seymour Chatman, ed. *Literary Style: A Symposium.* London and New York, Oxford UP, pp. 241–259.

Ohmann, Richard (1972a) "Speech, Literature and the Space Between." *New Literary History* 4(1), pp. 47–63.

Ohmann, Richard (1972b) "Instrumental Style: Notes on the Theory of Speech as Action." In Braj Kachru and Herbert Stahlke, eds. *Current Trends in Stylistics.* Edmonton, Linguistic Research, pp. 115–141.

Ohmann, Richard (1973) "Literature as Act." In Seymour Chatman, ed. *Approaches to Poetics.* New York, Columbia UP, pp. 81–107.

Ohmann, Richard (1978). "The Social Definition of Literature." In Paul Hernadi, ed. *What is Literature?* Bloomington, Indiana UP, pp. 89–101.

Pavis, Patrice (1980) "Dire et faire au théâtre: L'Action parlée dans les stances du *Cid." Etudes littéraires,* 13(3), pp. 515–538.

Petrey, Sandy (1984) "Speech Acts in Society: Fish, Felman, Austin and God." *Texte* 3, pp. 43–61.

Petrey, Sandy (1988a) "The Realist Speech Act: Mimesis, Performance and the Facts in Fiction." *Neohelicon* 15(2), pp. 9–29.

Petrey, Sandy (1988b) *Realism and Revolution: Balzac, Stendhal, Zola and the Performances of History.* Ithaca, Cornell UP.

Porter, Joseph A. (1979) *The Drama of Speech Acts: Shakespeare's Lancastrian Tetralogy.* Berkeley, University of California Press.

Powell, Mava Jo. (1985) "Conceptions of Literal Meaning in Speech Act Theory." *Philosophy and Rhetoric* 18(3), pp. 133–157.

Pratt, Mary Louise (1977) *Toward a Speech-Act Theory of Literary Discourse.* Bloomington, Indiana UP.

Pratt, Mary Louise (1981) "The Ideology of Speech-Act Theory." *Centrum* New Series 1(1), pp. 5–18.

Prince, Albert (1986) "Dramatic Speech Acts: A Reconsideration." In Rivers (1986) pp. 147–158.

Ricoeur, Paul (1981a) "The Model of the Text: Meaningful Action Considered as a Text." In his *Hermeneutics and the Human Sciences.* Cambridge, Cambridge UP, pp. 197–221.

Ricoeur, Paul (1981b) "Mimesis and Representation." *Annals of Scholarship* 11(3), pp. 15–32.

Rivers, Elias. (1983) *Quixotic Scriptures: Essays on the Textuality of Spanish Literature.* Bloomington, Indiana UP.

Rivers, Elias (ed.) (1986) *Things Done with Words: Speech Acts in Hispanic Drama.* Newark, Juan de la Cuesta.

Rivers, Elias (1989) "The *Comedia* as Discursive Action." In Dian Fox et al, eds. *Studies in Honor of Bruce W. Wardropper.* Newark, Juan de la Cuesta, pp. 249–256.

Rubenstein, Jill (1986) " 'For the Ovaltine had Loosened her Tongue': Failures of Speech in Barbara Pym's *Less Than Angels.*" *Modern Fiction Studies* 32(4), pp. 573–580.

Russell, Bertrand (1905) "On Denoting." *Mind* 14, pp. 479–493.

Savona, Jeannette Laillou (1980) "Narration et actes de parole dans le texte dramatique." *Etudes littéraires* 13(3), pp. 471–493.

Schneider, Monique (1981) "The Promise of Truth—The Promise of Love." *Diacritics* 11(3), pp. 27–38.

Searle, John R. (1969) *Speech Acts: An Essay in the Philosophy of Language.* Cambridge, Cambridge UP.

Searle, John R. (1977) "Reiterating the Differences: A Reply to Derrida." *Glyph* 1, pp. 198–208.

Searle, John R. (1979) *Expression and Meaning: Studies in the Theory of Speech Acts.* Cambridge, Cambridge UP.

Searle, John R. (1983a) *Intentionality: An Essay in the Philosophy of Mind.* Cambridge, Cambridge UP.

Searle, John R. (1983b) Review of Jonathan Culler, *On Deconstruction. New York Review of Books*, October 27, pp. 74–79.

Smith, Barbara Herrnstein (1975) "Actions, Fictions, and the Ethics of Interpretation." *Centrum* 3(2), pp. 117–120.

Spivak, Gayatri Chakravorty (1980) "Revolutions that as yet Have no Model: Derrida's 'Limited Inc.' " *Diacritics* 10(4), pp. 29–49.

Steinmann, Martin Jr. (1975) "Perlocutionary Acts and the Interpretation of Literature." *Centrum* 3(2), pp. 112–116.

Steinmann, Martin Jr. (1978) "Professor Martland on What it Means to Say Literature Represents 'Nothing.' " *Centrum* 6(2), pp. 121–127.

Tanaka, Ronald (1972) "Action and Meaning in Literary Theory." *Journal of Literary Semantics* 1, pp. 41–56.

van Dijk, Teun A. (1975) "Action, Action Description and Narrative." *New Literary History* 6(2), pp. 273–294.

Woodmansee, Martha (1978) "Speech-Act Theory and the Perpetuation of the Doctrine of Literary Autonomy." *Centrum* 6(2), pp. 75–89.

Yunes, Eliana (1986) "Vérité, pouvoir et propagande politique." *Degrés* 45, pp. 91–98.

Index